ENSIGNS AND ECHOES

To Bob & Claudine

Thankyou for looking after us. We both enjoyed our visit, especially the fabulous artwork.

best wishes

Steve - Lynne
Nicholas

Petty Officer S.J. Nicholas. Falklands, 1984.

Ensigns and Echoes

Steve Nicholas

Copyright © Steve Nicholas, 2002

First published in 2002 on behalf of the author
by Scotforth Books,
Carnegie House,
Chatsworth Road,
Lancaster LA1 4SL,
England
Tel: +44(0)1524 840111
Fax: +44(0)1524 840222
email: carnegie@provider.co.uk
Publishing and book sales: www.carnegiepub.co.uk
Book production: www.wooof.net

All rights reserved.
Unauthorised duplication
contravenes existing laws.

British Library Cataloguing-in-Publication data
A catalogue record for this book is available from the British Library

ISBN 1-904244-04-1

Typeset in Bell 11 on 13 by
Carnegie Publishing

Printed and bound in the UK by
The Cromwell Press, Wiltshire

To my wife, Gwen

Contents

	Illusrations	ix
	Introducion	1
Chapter I	Chatham	3
Chapter II	The Tyne	11
Chapter III	Royal Navy 1975–81	19
Chapter IV	Fearless and the Falklands, 1981–83	31
Chapter V	On the Move 1983–84	49
Chapter VI	RN – End of the Line, 1984–89	59
Chapter VII	CI Shipping, February 1989 to June 1990	75
Chapter VIII	Passengers, June 1990 to September 1993	91
Chapter IX	Snow Boats and Sweden	99
Chapter X	Container Boats, Germans and India	119
Chapter XI	Training and Tankers	127
Chapter XII	Ashore	137
	List of Subscribers	143

Illustrations

Petty Officer S.J. Nicholas. Falklands, 1984	*frontispiece*
My great grandfather and my grandfather	4
Chief Petty Officer, James W.L. Nicholas	5
RFA Sir Tristram in Bluff Cove 1982	39
Me and my mechanic	40
Bahia Pariso. Argentine Red Cross ship	42
MV Scirocco Universal in Egion, Greece, 14 March 1990	78
Gavin Swadel and I, 2nd mate Scirocco Universal, 1989	82
Christmas Dinner on Scirocco Universal	83
Gwen, Up a Crane	84
Gwen Steering with Bill Laverick	84
Gwen kitted-up with safety belt	84
Gwen and Third Engineer's wife at Pompeii	86
Panama Canal, 1990	87
MV Snow Crystal	100
First Engineer, John Hagan	101
MV Snow Crystal Control Room	102
My son David	102
MV Snow Drift	105
Captain Bill Lockie and I on a 650cc Moto Guzzi Motorcycle	107
Me on motorcycle	107

ENSIGNS AND ECHOES

Table Mountain	112
Capetown Drydock	114
Climbing Table Mountain, Lions Head from above	116
Me underneath the Lion's Head	116
Tadeusz Misiuro, Chief Officer, MV Snow Drift	117
San Pedro, Los Angeles 1997	120
Christmas Day 1998 on MV Tiger	124
Michael at sea with Maersk	128
My Family	129
MV Autosun in Tsuneishi, Japan, December 2000	138
Indian Ocean	140

Introduction

This book is based on the last twenty-six years of my seagoing career, but more than that it is the story of my family, the people I have met, and the ships they sailed on. A number of people over the years have told me to write it all down and this is the result. My intention is to provide a well balanced view, informing and I hope entertaining.

It is my intention to provide something for everyone, a little history to begin with, followed up by several chapters on the Royal Navy which occupied thirteen years of my life and then the 'Merchant Navy' which I will do my best to define.

There are gaps; I have left out large amounts to avoid duplication. Whilst it may seem that a life spent constantly travelling abroad may look glamorous there has been a lot of tedium. My present employment involves me in attending several vessels a year in various parts of the world for short periods necessitating many flights. A book based on recording the facilities in Amsterdam or Heathrow airports would be dull indeed.

The most important factor is the people I have encountered, sailors, soldiers, dockers, ships agents, engineering contractors, pilots and various owners of bars and nightclubs and their clientele. This really is their story and I have incorporated several of their tales in the book. In this respect I cannot assure total accuracy but where a story is involved it is presented as such. The rest is my own experience, how I saw things; again I have no doubt that my colleagues will disagree with me on certain aspects. My answer to that is that they write their own book, which could turn out to be very interesting. Some company's names have been omitted, as the name is not relevant. I have tried to keep the technical jargon to a minimum as what was fixed and when is not in my opinion of wide interest and has been included only where it has been relevant to the operation of the vessel.

ENSIGNS AND ECHOES

Photographs have all been from family sources and previously unpublished, including Falklands War photographs taken by my camera.

S. J. Nicholas
Bedlington
Northumberland

CHAPTER I

Chatham

SAPPER JAMES NICHOLAS, a Shropshire lad, had joined the Army, an innocent enough thing to do but this was a defining moment in my family's history. During the Boer War the Royal Engineers sailed off to South Africa. He returned having suffered from an affliction commonly known as trench fever; his daughter Norah (one of twelve children) rather unkindly attributed his return to blatant malingering.

Whatever the real reason he returned to Brompton Barracks in Gillingham, Kent, married Minnie a Yorkshire lass (then in service) and they settled in Chatham. He worked in the Royal Dockyard on building works whilst Minnie struggled to maintain a growing brood of children in a two-bedroom terraced house. As the children grew they were farmed out along the street and as the boys attained the age of fifteen they were marched down to the dockyard and enrolled as apprentices.

My grandfather (his son) enrolled as apprentice shipwright in 1918 building and repairing ships of an immense Royal Navy that after four years of war the nation could no longer afford. Unfortunately the Navy was committed in several areas around the world, shipbuilding was scaled down, ships were sold and larger vessels retained for many years longer than previously envisaged.

At the end of his apprenticeship there were simply no jobs to go to and so James W. L. Nicholas joined the Royal Navy in 1926. He stayed for over twenty years, attaining the position of Chief Petty Officer Shipwright before returning at the end of the Second World War to the Royal dockyard in 1948. He served on the cruisers HMS *Emerald*, HMS *Enterprise* and HMS *Cornwall*.

In 1942 HMS *Cornwall*, a County class cruiser, approached what seemed to be a merchant ship in the Indian Ocean. As they came closer the *Pinguin*, a German armed merchant cruiser, formerly named *Kandelfels* (which had sunk or captured twenty-eight merchant vessels), and

ENSIGNS AND ECHOES

3rd from left Sapper J Nicholas – my great grandfather
2nd from left C.P.O. J W L Nicholas – my grandfather

owned by the Hansa Line dropped her false covers and opened fire with her 6 × 5.9-inch guns. Chaos ensued with the *Cornwall* sustaining some damage, temporarily knocking out the gun control system, turning then opening fire on the unfortunate *Pinguin*, which promptly blew up and sank. *Pinguin* had been a menace in the Indian ocean and had sunk Granddad, after 2 years and 10 months on the ship. He returned on the *City of Colombo* and came home leaving the *Cornwall* in the Far East.

As it turned out this was a lucky escape as the *Cornwall* was sunk with the loss of 191 men when with HMS *Dorsetshire* they were attacked by Japanese aircraft. With no air cover the ships were doomed. Time after time when ships without air cover were attacked by aircraft, whether German or Japanese, the outcome was invariably the same. HMS *Enterprise* and two destroyers picked up the survivors. Lessons taught are not always lessons learned and, forty years later, I found myself in a similar position. At least in 1942 the excuse that we did not know could be applied. The problem being that in a democracy, spending money on defence is invariably unpopular and, as with the beginning of the Second World War, the government and treasury were more concerned with saving money than making sure we did not fall behind with technology or strategy; this proved very costly in the long term.

The grief felt by granddad having lost so many shipmates can only be imagined; forty years later a friend of mine (removed from HMS *Sheffield* with a broken leg before the War) was shattered when the ship was sunk in the Falklands, by aircraft, without air cover. He was put on the switchboards answering telephone calls from anxious relatives, some of whom he knew. The cruelty of some people knows no bounds and many turned on him with the words, 'Why weren't you there?'. This was particularly cruel and it would not surprise me if Granddad had had to endure the same venomous taunts.

The war dragged on, James now had three children of his own who were being bombed by the Germans, with monotonous regularity back home in Chatham. On 6/6/1944 the first minesweeper on the D-Day landings was HMS *Pelorous*, an Algerines class minesweeper. She did her job and hit a mine on 10 July injuring Granddad who had to be wrapped in bandages as he had some broken ribs. The Captain whose name was Nelson had been chastised for sending a signal saying that 'Nelson was in the van'. The *Pelorous* survived for a great many years after, having been sold to the South African Navy as the SAS *Pietermaritzburg*. In 1995 I arrived in Capetown two weeks after they sank her as an artificial reef off Simonstown after attempts to restore her were deemed pointless due to her advanced state of decay. The book *They Led The Way* by Jack Williams states that the ship was to be saved but sadly time ran out.

Chief Petty Officer, James W.L. Nicholas

(my grandfather)

In 1946 James found himself working on HMS *Argus*, the first aircraft carrier which had by then become a floating repair and maintenance centre. He left the Navy soon afterwards and returned to the dockyard from where he had started latterly building submarines.

At the same time my mother Enid's brother, Eric Higgins, was serving in the Far East on the aircraft carriers HMS *Indomitable* and HMS *Indefatigable*. The Royal Naval aircraft carriers with their armoured decks proved extremely successful in warding off kamikaze attempts. Eric, suffering from prickly heat, returned to work for Short Bros, building aircraft in Rochester Kent.

The time came for my father to be marched down to the dockyard at the age of fifteen where he took the dockyard exam and duly became an Electrical Apprentice. His younger brother, Robert, joined the Royal Navy and his cousin, Allan Jarrett, the Merchant Navy.

Allan joined the training ship *Vindicatrix* in 1948 as a Boy Seaman, where they woke up to the call 'Rise and shine for the White Star Line'. After training in the most awful of conditions on this ageing hulk of a sailing ship he then travelled to Southampton to join the *Athlone Castle*. They sailed for South Africa where the young Allan had his first taste of Coca Cola. He told me that the Bosun had warned all the boys that it was more harmful than alcohol and to leave it alone. Allan's stories, as with so many other of my relatives, could fill a book by themselves but some of his tales must be recounted, although I must admit that I could never retell them like Allan. He had listened to all the stories of his uncle Jim (Granddad) and did not believe one word.

One particular story concerned a drunken incident where a bewildered Jim woke up in a four-poster bed being served coffee. He had been picked up and looked after by Mr Skinner who turned out to be South Africa's premier wood importer. Allan investigated this story and it all turned out to be true. The stories occupied Allan's mind. Eventually when his ship docked in Durban he visited Skinners along with another boy. They asked for Mr Skinner who, on hearing that he was Jim Nicholas's nephew, looked after them for five days with trips to the theatre and all manner of chocolate and nylon stockings which he brought back home. Allan left Union Castle, where the unnecessary discipline had not endeared him to the company. Further jobs came on the *Ashbell Hubbard*, an old coal burner of 1,700 tons; they took broom handles to Aalborg. He missed another vessel, the *June Crest* despite chasing the ship in the Pilot Boat in Tilbury. This nearly landed Allan in jail, as once signed on it was an offence to miss the vessel.

The next trip on the *Empire Baltic* was a memorable one. She was a Tank Landing Ship with bow doors fixed with large bottlescrews. She brought back tanks and all manner of military vehicles to Tilbury from Germany. She had been built as LST 3519 by Canadian Vickers, Montreal and completed in September 1945. Due to a navigational error the ship wandered out of the swept channel and hit a mine. Allan described the ship heeling right over, one of the propellers was blown off, the lights went out and his head was gashed. The tug refused to enter the minefield so the engineers managed to repair one engine and, with Allan at the wheel, they nosed out of the minefield. He described the hull of the ship resembling corrugated iron in the dry dock.

He came back to England as passenger on the *Empire Doric* and went to work on the *Royal Sovereign* doing day trips to the coast of France out of Dover. He then embarked on the *Fort Esperance*, a 7,000-ton Freighter. This ship was another wreck. The accommodation aft was split between Europeans and Arabs, the cook was Polish and the food rotten. The stories of the *Fort Esperance* go on and on. During a storm they had to trim coal; or run out. The Arabs refused to work so the Captain, with gun in hand, threatened to shoot the lot if they didn't. Allan describes the dingy atmosphere of unbearable heat with so much clarity you would have thought it happened yesterday. They sailed from Suez around Africa, Dar Es Salaam, Freetown, Wari and Takoradi, before ending up in Newcastle upon Tyne where the ship was strike bound.

Allan left the Merchant Navy and, after working for a small Engineering firm in Dartford, was called up for national service. In the RAF he was amazed by the food that everyone else moaned about, did not see the point of marching round in circles and after emerging as top all-round recruit was posted on a drill instructors' course. This was resented by Allan who after having been an AB in the Merchant Navy requested to be posted to the Marine section. This was granted after Allan had accosted his commanding officer. A spell in Northern Ireland followed, then he was posted to Singapore. As cox'n of a 47½-foot launch (number 1647) he towed Sunderland flying boats, a most hazardous thing to do by all accounts due to the tendency of the aircraft to drag the boat under the spinning props. He also took Gurkhas up into the jungle and ferried numerous dignitaries including Sir Robert Black, Governor of Singapore. After Singapore, as far as this book goes the story ends, but Allan, now an energetic seventy year old, has turned his hand to many enterprises.

After his apprenticeship my father John Dudley Nicholas had to do his national service and joined the Royal Navy as an Artificer Apprentice. The ships he sailed on for two years were ex-Second World War vessels long past their retirement age. The Second World War had now finally put an end to the ailing British Empire, but global responsibilities were still immense. Conflict around the world continued. Some people would have had trouble defining the end of one war and the beginning of another. Since 1945, Palestine, Korea, Suez, Malaya, Borneo, the Falklands, Yugoslavia and the Gulf War of 1990 have all involved the Royal Navy including numerous humanitarian missions around the world. Royal dockyards were still in existence in Singapore until the 1960s, Hong Kong until 1997. Gibraltar is now privatised, as are our own yards in Rosyth and Plymouth.

The year 1956 found my father on HMS *Leeds Castle*, now designated as a frigate. It had been an ex-Second World War Corvette which my Mother still describes after she visited my father on board as being held together with cockroaches holding hands. They were nearly sunk by HMS *Belfast* during a night exercise due to being in the wrong place. Her other claim to fame was having taken part in the film *Cockleshell Heroes* (playing the part of a German destroyer). Finally Suez erupted and the *Leeds Castle* nearly went but was spared. His next ship was HMS *Obdurate* a Second World War veteran from the battle of the Barents Sea. Dad left the Navy and went back into the dockyard, taking part in refits of, amongst others, HMS *Petard*, the ship that captured U571 and the Enigma code. A recent film of the event puts the victory in the hands of the American Navy but in fact there were no American ships present.

Dad rose to foreman, took and passed his Inspector's exams, planning to move to Canada where one branch of the family was already well established. Great Uncle George had ended up in the Royal Canadian Mounted Police (nicknamed by the family as the Chatham Mountie) and became governor of Sioux Saint Marie in Ontario. In 1966 a position arose on the River Tyne as Overseer, thoughts of Canada faded and my family moved north. I was eight years old.

From a once large family concentrated in Chatham everyone seemed on the move. Uncle Robert married in Scotland and also moved north serving the rest of his RN career of twenty-seven years in Rosyth. He used to send me pictures of the ships he was on and I still have a photograph of HMS *Defender*, a Daring class destroyer. I briefly did some training on HMS *Diamond*, another Daring class, in 1975 which was by then laid up and used as a training ship. His son James, now an Air Engineer in the Royal Air Force, speaks with a distinctly Scottish accent. Other branches of the family disappeared to Australia, Canada and South Africa, sometimes with no word of warning.

From the 1940s and 1950s, with a busy dockyard and a still considerable fleet, it must have been inconceivable that half a century later Chatham Dockyard would be a museum piece. Once on a par with the now scaled-down Portsmouth and the reduced and privatised Plymouth, Chatham is a shadow of its former self. HMS *Victory* was built there, as were various Submarines including HMC Sm *Ojibwa* for the Canadian Navy, which my father had worked on and I had visited in Gibraltar in 1985.

The last ship to be built in Chatham for the Royal Navy was HMS *Leopard*, a frigate in the mid-1960s.

Work was concentrated on repair; the skilled workers left and Chatham finally closed its RN Barracks (HMS *Pembroke*) in the early 1980s. I attended a leadership course in 1980 at *Pembroke* which was by then the RN school for catering, but this has now been moved to a joint services catering school.

My mother's father had worked in the dockyard as a Coppersmith, in fact so many people were employed there that everyone in Chatham and Gillingham either worked there or were related to someone who did. Home to the Navy and the Army in its hey day, it must have been teeming with humanity, a large number being added to by my prolific family.

We can never escape the past it is all around us, the decisions taken by those members of the family mentioned dictated what I did and to some extent my own sons. Echoes from the past keep resurfacing. My last ship in the Royal Navy was the next HMS *Leeds Castle*, my position Petty Officer in charge of the Electrical department. I visited the old China Fleet club in Hong Kong in 1980 not long before it was demolished to make way for high-rise blocks. My grandfather had frequented this establishment in the 1930s whilst on the China station on HMS *Enterprise*, a cruiser. One of his stories concerned a rather dangerous attempt to swim back to the ship, which was at anchor. Having missed the boat he swam into the middle of Durban harbour, climbing onto a buoy and shouting at the ship, *'Enterprise, Enterprise'* until a disgruntled duty watch turned on the searchlights to find out what the commotion was all about. It can only be imagined what the Captain thought on being told his Chief Shipwright was currently manning a buoy and please could he put out a boat to retrieve him.

CHAPTER II

The Tyne

IN 1966 CLUTCHING MY TEDDY BEAR I found myself on a train heading towards Newcastle upon Tyne. Our cat, a particularly large grey moggy known as Sparky, was trying to fight his way out of the cardboard carrying box we had obtained from the vet. As the journey neared its end, claws frantically scrabbling at the box appeared, accompanied by the most dreadful noise. A tranquillizer had not had the slightest effect on the cantankerous feline and soothing words from my Mum had little impact either.

My father had of course already been in Newcastle for some time, looking for a house and familiarising himself with his new position.

People can have very strange attitudes I was regularly informed, on occasion by adults, that I would be living on top of a coal tip and breathing noxious fumes to the accompaniment of factory whistles. My father told a different tale of long beaches, majestic castles, rivers and streams and a beautiful landscape. This county of Northumberland is my home and having lived all over the country, I have no desire to go anywhere else. We had moved to Whitley Bay and at first I suffered a little disappointment. We had gone to the beach at high tide and my promised beach was not there. As the tide receded and I scrabbled across the rocks at Saint Mary's Island I soon found an enthusiasm for the place that has never left me.

What I had not bargained for was the other children's dislike of my accent; for my part I mainly did not understand much of what they said. When one of the teachers referred to a 'fillum' instead of film I quickly became confused. For much of my time at school in the North-East I became increasingly isolated. As more people moved up from Chatham to Newcastle I found that my parents' friends were not the parents of my school associates and I lived a kind of double life. This continued until I was twelve years old.

One of the first ships I visited on the Tyne in connection with my father was the *Scharnhorst*, an ex-RN Black Swan class frigate, sold to the Germans and handed over on the Tyne. At the age of eight I was already keenly interested in naval affairs and history. At a party thrown by the German officers I was introduced to the Captain who was standing in front of two previous *Scharnhorsts*; my parents were a little embarrassed when to prove my knowledge I asked if those ships had been sunk by the Royal Navy. I knew that one had been sunk in 1914 the other in 1943. It is to the German Captain's eternal credit that he made light of my gaffe and was extremely courteous at all times. All the children were looked after very well by the officers who took turns to entertain us.

A high point in 1968 came when I got out of school early one day with a friend and we were whisked off to the launching of HMS *Bacchante*, a Leander class frigate, which my father had helped to build. The *Bacchante* has now been sold to the New Zealand Navy, one of several navies who snapped up the Leanders as they were discarded by our own. With a double-barrelled 4.5 inch Mk 6 gun, two Quadruple Seacat anti-aircraft missile launchers and a triple-barrelled anti-submarine mortar, together with various Oerlikens, they were good, well-built, general purpose frigates which were the backbone of the Royal Navy for several years.

My uncle Robert was a Chief Petty Officer on HMS *Andromeda* one of twenty-six Leanders purchased by the Royal Navy. Navies all over the world bought them including the Netherlands and Chile. During my last visit to Valparaiso in 1994 I saw several Leanders and County class guided missile destroyers such as ex-HMS *Norfolk* (which as a member of the Mobile Fleet Maintenance Group I had worked on in 1979), and ex-HMS *Fife* another ship Uncle Robert had served on. Most noticeably in the Mediterranean he had been involved in putting out a fire on the *Fife*. *Norfolk* had been built on the Tyne, the ships were solid and well built and it is a pity that ships of the Royal Navy have been proved not to be so well designed and constructed as these long-lived reliable vessels.

I went down to the Tyne to visit a number of vessels my father worked on including the Royal Fleet Auxiliary vessels *Green Rover*, *Grey Rover*, *Blue Rover* and the LSL *Sir Tristram* of which much more will be heard in a later chapter.

At the age of twelve I joined Whitley Bay Sea Cadet Corps, having outgrown Blyth Lifeguard and swimming club. I enjoyed swimming but the SCC gave me so much more. The unit was ably commanded by Lt CDR Ken Caslaw SCC RNR and today is commanded by his son Paul. The number of activities on offer was amazing; within one year I had travelled to Portsmouth staying on HMS *Ramehead* for a week, hiked across the Northumbrian hills with Dougie Turner the hiking instructor and worked on the unit's Motorboat, the MTRV 'McGregor'. The *Ramehead* was later replaced by HMS *Ulster*. Every Thursday we would go swimming in Byker swimming baths, Wednesday and Friday were parade and instruction nights and we would often go shooting in Tynemouth TA centre. We played football and for two consecutive years I captained the adventure training team. In 1972 I became dreadfullyly seasick having been taken to sea on HMS *Northumbria*, a Ton class minesweeper which had a particularly odd motion.

The 'McGregor' was built in 1939 by Thorneycrofts in Southampton for the Royal Navy, the prefix standing for Motor Torpedo Recovery Vessel. She is still on the Tyne today having been sunk three times by being rammed in various incidents. There were many years when we just stayed at our mooring in North Shields by the fish quay. Every now and again we would head up the Tyne to Newburn, on one occasion staying overnight, myself and another cadet cramped in the focsle locker. I loved pottering up the Tyne and was not too worried about the neverending job of scraping seagull excrement from the decks; being moored next to a fish quay definitely had its disadvantages.

In 1973 I managed to get a chance to sail on the TS *Royalist*, a square-rigged, two-masted brigantine. At the time I was particularly worried by heights and whilst I approached the task with some bravado I was absolutely petrified about the prospect of climbing the 80-foot masts which I knew I would have to do. Rule number one is that it is OK to be scared.

Off I went to Portsmouth for my first foray abroad, joining the vessel in Gosport. Our one-week trip was to take us to such exotic locations as Braye in Alderney, Cherbourg then back to Portsmouth. To me at the time it seemed like an ocean voyage. My family never did go on foreign holidays and in fact still don't, whilst my future wife at the same time had travelled around Europe, and had been skiing in Norway. My greatest claim to fame in the travel stakes had been holidays in Scotland. What I did not realise until later was the significance of the trip in how it had subtly changed my perspective. I just about passed my Sail Training

Association offshore hand certificate but I must admit to preferring to look at the vessel alongside rather than be at sea, with the deck heeling over and the sea washing down the waist. Stuck up a mast in any kind of wind I found to be most unpleasant, though I endured. One annoying facet of life on the *Royalist* was the toilets, not so much the toilets but the strange things that people put in them. Signs around the heads clearly stated the procedure for flushing and proclaimed 'nothing, except the paper provided is to be put down the toilet unless it has been eaten first'. A simple request, unheeded by one gentleman at least. The inevitable happened, the heads blocked, a heavily soiled pair of underpants were removed with the hunt on as to who had perpetrated such a crime. It was obvious to me that the culprit was unlikely to own up. The said underpants, in a most unsanitary condition, were hung up above the mess room table for at least one day while we were berated for being all manner of creatures not worthy of our current good fortune. As I had not been the criminal I did not see the point of it all, as predicted no one owned up.

In Cherbourg I visited the *Malcolm Miller* which along with the *Winston Churchill* was relatively new. They have both recently been sold and I last saw a forlorn-looking *Malcolm Miller* in Southampton in November 2000 awaiting a buyer. As with so many of the vessels I have been on since, conditions were cramped and uncomfortable. I particularly remember one foggy day in the English Channel with the ship barely moving and wondering why I had been so enthusiastic about the vessel. It took some time before I realised how lucky I had been to be there and to fully appreciate what I had learned. The Captain's name was Francis Drake, and it only recently struck me that as my grandfather had sailed with Nelson so I had with Drake. I last saw the *Royalist* in the Solent in the year 2000 whilst entering Southampton on a Norwegian-flagged car carrier. Car carriers are extremely ugly whereas the *Royalist* was one of the best-looking vessels I have sailed on.

Between 1971 and my *Royalist* trip in 1973 I had visited several naval establishments. Notably the Royal Naval Air Stations in Lossiemouth (HMS *Fulmar* now RAF Lossiemouth) and RNAS Culdrose (HMS *Seahawk*) where I was winched up by Whirlwind 9 helicopters and generally given a good time with a hearty dose of naval discipline to go with it. It is unlikely that the vast majority of modern youth would be strong enough to take this discipline. So many times I hear young people hiding behind what they loosely term 'their rights'. It was abundantly clear to me that at the time I had no rights and the best thing to do would be to get on with what I was doing. The summer of 1973 passed quickly. In September I joined Amble County Secondary School's seamanship unit under the master, Mr Shawcross. He had been a Tanker Master and regularly poured contempt on the Royal Navy and Engineers who he referred to as plumbers. Out of fifteen boys in my class (no girls), six joined the Royal Navy, and one joined the Merchant Navy but two years later I saw him in HMS *Collingwood* having left his position as Radio Officer, and one went to join the trawlers in Hull. I never saw him again and often wonder if he ever did board a trawler, and if after the destruction of the fishing industry by Europe to the large benefit of Spanish fisherman, he still has a job.

A survey vessel had come into the Tyne and was to survey Amble Harbour. Two of us joined HMS *Enterprise*, the namesake of my grandfather's ship, in Newcastle and sailed up to Amble where we were shown how to take bearings and make notes on the charts. Most of us joining the RN went into technical positions. At Christmas Mr Shawcross would show us slides, pictures he had taken in the great lakes.

The Science master had been at D-Day on a cruiser as a midshipman in the RN. I have met a lot of people who were involved in that operation, which gives testament to the size of it. In the Sea Cadets one officer had commanded a landing craft, and later whilst living on the Isle of Wight it transpired that my next-door neighbour had served on HMS *Hawkins* another D-Day veteran. In 1989 whilst serving on a Merchant Vessel I met an ex ordnance artificer who had been on HMS *Ramillies*, a battleship which had bombarded German positions.

With a school motor boat (the *Seaquest*), a motor whaler and several small sailing dinghies in the boatyard we spent every Thursday on the water and sometimes worked in the evening. Mr Shawcross would make us row out to sea in the whaler, refusing to use the engine. We would also sail out of the Coquet on the *Seaquest* and using sextants would plot our position. The job I hated most was writing down the weather forecast; for'd lookout could also be most unpleasant in the winter in the North Sea, but Mr Shawcross insisted on it.

In 1974 I continued in Whitley Bay Sea Cadets at the weekends as I was away at school all week lodging with an elderly couple in Shilbottle. A course to HMS *Collingwood* in Electrics taught me more about Science in one week than a year in school. My father was by now First Lieutenant in the Sea Cadets and my Mother was also involved despite a serious illness.

On 8 November I took part in a parade for the visit of the Duke of Edinburgh where I was presented with the Gold Amateur Swimming Association Award. The day was most memorable for more than one reason – I met the young lady who was to become my wife. I also got the chance of showing off by dealing with a big lump of a lad who was annoying her. She was in the Girls' Nautical Training Corps, a kind of female equivalent of the Sea Cadets. They never benefited as much as the boys and I often thought it unfair that they did not get as much out of it as we boys did. As for myself, joint manoeuvres would have been severely distracting, political correctness is one thing hormones quite another. The main problem with the girls was that they had no female officers who could do things. The female officers had a Girl Guide approach and although they were respected for giving up their time they were, in most ways, unprepared to deal with young ladies of a more adventurous disposition (most of the girls at that time while not resenting found that to be constrictive). Most if not all the men felt uneasy about the girls.

Mick Forrester looked after the boats and trained us in our rowing competitions on the Tyne and at Ashington where we used to spend weekends on the Wansbeck. Dougie Turner took us up Hellvelyn in the Lake District and the Cheviots in Northumberland; my father instructed swimming and Ken Caslaw took us for shooting with the unit's .22 rifles. In later years having been Chairman of the civilian committee in the Air Training Corps I was aware that sometimes adult male instructors could unwittingly put themselves in positions which on occasion can lead to charges of inappropriate behaviour with adolescent female cadets. Whilst I would not describe myself as sexist I would not enjoy instructing young girls and have for that reason refused to go into uniform for the benefit of teenagers, but I have every respect for those who do. In these days of political correctness I would be seen as some type of misogynistic beast if I joined an institution and requested not to teach girls.

At the end of 1974 I was totally unaware of how much my life would change in the coming year. My father accepted a position as Chief Apprentice Training Officer for the Ministry of Defence in Bath, by which time I had fallen for Gwen Howe, the young lady I mentioned at the Duke of Edinburgh parade. I took my entrance examination in Gunner House in Newcastle, failing to achieve the mark for Artificer. I was offered the position of Junior Electrical Mechanic and given the date of joining the Navy as 16/9/1975. Mr Shawcross described this as a real waste as I had taken exams in Seamanship and Navigation. A problem with my right eye meant that I was unlikely to get a job on deck anyway.

By the time I joined the Navy we were living in Bath, I was instructed to travel to Plymouth where I would be picked up on the Cornish side of the Torpoint ferry and taken to HMS *Raleigh*. The initial training lasted for 6 weeks after which time I would get further training in HMS *Collingwood*.

CHAPTER III

Royal Navy 1975–81

THE ROYAL NAVY was no shock for me; I had lived with naval discipline in its more extreme forms on a gunnery course two years earlier in HMS *Excellent*. I was made class leader and instantly became the most unpopular boy in the class. I could see through the shouted orders and realised why things were taught in this way. If you are training people to fight, which is what the RN is all about, there is no room for trying to mollycoddle people. If one person on the course failed we all failed in some way. Only two people dropped out of my class.

I have always abhorred bullying and one particularly nasty ritual which involved victimisation of a so-called crab, by which I mean a dirty individual, had nothing to do with hygiene and everything to do with picking on the weakest. I stopped this in my mess and banned members of other classes from entering my mess with the intention of promoting this ritual. I was most surprised that my classmates rebelled against my decision; they obviously privately longed for some excitement. I alienated myself further when I suggested that whilst they may have homosexual tendencies I did not. As homosexuality was then illegal in the armed forces this promoted fury. In years to come as I occasionally met former classmates I was surprised that many still held a grudge against me. That I was not perhaps the most democratic of leaders was true, but democracy was rightly discouraged in the RN. What surprised me was that they could not see that I was only sixteen myself.

My parents and Gwen came down for the passing out parade and that night with money collected we took all the parents, relatives and our Petty Officer Instructor PO Broad for a night out. The training was not bad, lots of emphasis on cleaning, drill, a spot of shooting the SLR 7.62mm rifles and the gas chamber. I remember one occasion when a sadistic Senior Rate made us run up and down a hill before we put on respirators and entered the chamber where we were exposed to CS gas.

I knew this was necessary to test for leaks, however the purpose of the running was to open the pores on our skin through sweating; this was particularly sore and most unnecessary. In retrospect I can now say that the training I received in no way prepared me for being on a ship. Whilst being perfectly capable of marching round a parade ground, serving as Electrical Mechanic on a warship was a different matter. I left Collingwood in June 1976 as a Junior Ordnance Electrical Mechanic 2nd Class.

In February 1976, whilst being between courses, a few of us were taken to HMS *Royal Arthur* the Petty Officers' leadership school. We were taken up the Black Mountains where one lad suddenly collapsed with breathing difficulties. It was very cold so we wrapped him up and I went down the mountain to get help. The Chief Petty Officer and myself walked for miles to get the Land Rover and on the way back collided with a maniac in a Mini. The Chief braked and stopped but the Mini was travelling way too fast and bounced off the Land Rover with a completely destroyed engine. It was some time before we picked up the others having to sort out the lunatic in the Mini and his irate girlfriend. The chap with breathing difficulties was taken to an army hospital where it was discovered that he did not breathe efficiently. I later heard he was cured, and was explained as too long a time spent in front of the TV.

As a volunteer for submarines, I then embarked on Submarine training in HMS *Dolphin*. I wanted to go on a diesel boat, one of the ageing O&P class submarines. The course lasted six weeks which included escape practice in the wet tank. The tank was 100 feet deep and escapes were carried out from pods in the side from first 30 feet then 60 feet and finally in a suit from the bottom of the tank at 100 feet. I passed the course but to my dismay I was selected for Polaris submarines and was sent to HMS *Sultan*, the RN School for marine engineering. To sail from Faslane, remain under water for six to twelve weeks before returning to Faslane was not my idea of fun. Depression set in and I failed my Nuclear Propulsion Short Course.

There was some shame in being thrown off the course but in retrospect it was probably the best thing. I was, in common parlance, returned to general service.

In October 1976 I joined the first ship that I was ever to be paid for working on. HMS *Bristol* the only Type-82 ever built for the RN was being refitted in Portsmouth after being severely damaged by a serious fire. This was the start of many a lazy day, for we were going nowhere;

I was less than effective and at seventeen clueless in what was expected of me. The ship was a real mess, engine rooms had been burnt out as had accommodation and the ship would not sail for over a year. My dreams of travel were shattered. We lived in the RN barracks in Portsmouth, HMS *Nelson* and I wish I had known that these days would be the most trouble free in the Navy, with zero responsibility and absolutely zero expected of me.

Later in 1977 I was transferred to barrack guard for three months. Portsmouth was teeming with sailors from all over the world for the Queen's Silver Jubilee Fleet Review. Our cells were absolutely full of drunks, we were regularly turned out as after the pubs emptied and the nightclubs threw sailors out we were deluged with a stream of drunken sailors attempting to steal hats and threatening violence to the Officer of the Day. During the day we were beset with tourists, usually Americans, asking for HMS *Victory*. The washing machines were taken out of the blocks because some idiot threw one out of the window narrowly missing the Padre.

Another annoying incident involved a bicycle parked against the block with a full saddlebag. The owner did not remember having a full saddlebag and the bomb disposal squad were sent for. We had to clear a high-rise accommodation block full of drunken lunatics whose attitude was 'If it blows it blows, I am not getting out of bed!' The bomb squad put a small charge on the bag and promptly blew up his laundry which he had forgotten about.

On 12 May 1977 I took an examination and was promoted to Ordnance Electrical Mechanic 1st class: after nineteen months I had improved a little. A winter spent sorting out the upper deck lighting had meant that I was at least half useful. We were still not mobile having by now spent 19 months in dry dock and alongside still being repaired.

The Bristol was an odd vessel, a test bed for new weapons and an experiment with propulsion systems. She was the first ship to have the new single-barrelled 4.5 inch Mk 8 gun, the first to be fitted with Seadart and Ikara missile systems. She was also fitted with the more conventional triple-barrelled anti-submarine mortar and 20mm Oerliken anti-aircraft guns. There was a flight deck but no hanger and the ship bristled with aerials. The propulsion consisted of two steam turbines and two Rolls Royce gas turbines acting on two shafts. She also had six stabilisers and a generating plant capable of producing 9Mw of power.

ENSIGNS AND ECHOES

We went to Portland, and stayed and stayed, back to Portsmouth then Portland; exercise was piled upon exercise. I started to wonder if there were any other ports in the world, preferably sunny. On one occasion we actually achieved 38 knots; standing on the flight deck I could see it above me as she dug her stern into the sea. The inevitable happened and during yet another replenishment at sea exercise we collided with a Royal Fleet Auxiliary supply ship. I was eating steak and kidney pie in the junior rates dining hall at the time when suddenly there was a crunch followed by a frantic tannoy command to close up to emergency stations. Before we came into Portsmouth the Chief Shipwright had to construct a wooden cover to hide the gash in the side. The collision had dismounted a small davit crane and hydraulic oil flowed over the deck. Visits to Dunkirk and Liverpool were noticeable by their mediocrity, except for one incident in Liverpool when my friend Taff saw a boy running away with a Lollipop Lady's stick. Rushing to the rescue he rugby tackled the unfortunate boy and returned the stick only to be told that the child was her son and he was only taking it back home. Taff never lived that one down. We sailed up to Kirkwall in the Orkney Islands and laid a wreath on the mast of HMS *Royal Oak*, sunk in the Second World War at Scapa Flow with several civilians onboard. As part of the Standing Naval Force Atlantic we were with several navies including a Chilean vessel. A sports day was held on a school field and in driving rain I played softball with Chilean sailors, which we won.

Also in 1977 I put out my first fire on the starboard auxiliary boiler with MEM Fell. The *Bristol* was prone to fires and breakdowns, the weapons often would not work properly and the gearbox problems must have been a nightmare for the manufacturer's service engineers who seemed to reside permanently on the vessel. In later years I realised that the weapon system failures were not so much an inconvenience as a serious threat to our safety. Together with the absence of proper aircraft carriers which could operate F-4 Phantom and Buccaneers, the Navy's weapons fit, far from being the state of the art efficient systems we believed we had, was a mess. The Seadart was particularly fickle, as was the Ikara, an anti-submarine missile system from Australia that in over two and a half years was never fired. The 4.5 Mk 8 gun was, in my opinion, an inferior weapon to the Mk 6 although it required less people to man it. No point in saving numbers on a ship if it is less able to defend itself. The Navy too often listened to experts who, when all was said and done, were glorified salesmen. We would have fared better if we had purchased American systems which tended to work better than our own.

In 1978 I married Gwen, leaving the ship in Portland and getting married on 1 April in Whitley Bay. We moved into a married quarter in Gosport whereupon she became instantly pregnant. Orders came to proceed to the Caribbean and we sailed in August 1978. Our first port of call was Bermuda. After a little rough weather lasting for about three days the sky turned blue, the flying fish and dolphins appeared and the pace of life slowed. I also saw phosphorescence for the first time. Older hands told us it was because we were entering the Bermuda triangle, and we looked at the flashes of green light in the water with some consternation.

Bermuda was excellent; since the day I left in 1978 I have unfortunately never returned. I dived on the coral reefs seeing fish of radiant blue and striking red, friendly fish which swam unconcernedly past occasionally inspecting you. Bermuda is made up of a succession of islands joined by bridges. Whilst standing on one I looked into the water and saw a huge manta ray swim underneath looking almost prehistoric. It was the first time I had seen cacti growing wild and the beaches were almost white beneath the hot sun.

At that time we were berthed at Ireland Island at the end of a chain of islands. There was a small RN club there and a bar where we lounged on the grass drinking rum and cokes. A few brave souls rented mopeds; unfortunately to reach the ship it was necessary to drive down a hill and take a sharp left, failure to do so resulted in moped and rider getting very wet. The chap who rented these machines out must have suffered this to happen before as he returned in the morning with a diver and crane.

I loved Bermuda, and I must admit to being a little disappointed when we visited the Bahamas. Nassau was the first port and we berthed at the Straw Market. Nassau was more commercial and it was obvious to me that we were not made as welcome as we had been in Bermuda. In Freeport Grand Bahama a double-decker bus arrived at the ship to take us into town. There was a large cassino and a pub, neither of which we could afford to stay in long. I have visited Freeport since but did not venture ashore as I found it to be a waste of time with little to see. Next stop was West Palm Beach in Florida, then Maryport.

I took leave in Norfolk Virginia and Gwen flew across to spend some time with me. The US Navy treated us very well. We went to Washington DC and visited the museums of the Smithsonian Institute, getting cheap tickets for the Greyhound bus via their travel agent. The US Navy bases always had extremely good services, putting our own to shame. We were always told how we were the most professional navy in the world. One Admiral even sent a signal round the Fleet when people started to leave due to low pay and poor conditions that the Navy was a big club and how we enjoyed 'fun in the sun'. The majority of us treated this signal with contempt.

The mess deck I was living in was divided in two with thirty-three living on each side. My mess was 4J Starboard Mess; we had to queue for everything including pay. Every other Thursday the ship's company would line up around the passageways in alphabetical order to receive pay. I was pleased that one day all the banks were invited down to the ship and we all opened accounts so that our pay could be paid straight into the bank every month. Once a week we would get a film, a sheet would be hung up as a screen and if you arrived late you had to go behind the sheet and therefore the image was reversed. The films were often repeated and most of our leisure time was spent singing songs, writing home or playing uckers, a kind of ludo taken very seriously at the time and on occasion would end in blows and the table would have to be repaired again.

The mess was full of Electrical Sailors, maintainers and operators of various equipment. We had two Able Seaman, one of whom, Stan Sayers, I am indebted for kicking me into action. I was content to stay as I was until Stan gave me the lecture of a lifetime. So I studied and took a written and oral examination for Leading Ordnance Electrical Mechanic. I passed, but although I received more pay I was not recommended for promotion as my attitude needed adjustment. My oldest son David John Nicholas was born in 1979 and I had the privilege of witnessing his birth on 26 January. A Pakistani man waiting for his fifth child was getting attired as his wife was in labour. After the birth I was surprised to see him on a stretcher. He said 'I always faint, it's the emotion'. My knees were a bit wobbly but apart from that I was OK.

I took the exam for advancement in May 1979 and determined to improve. I left the *Bristol* in May 1979 for some leave then joined the Mobile Fleet Maintenance Group Portsmouth. Within two weeks of joining I flew with several others to Perth in Western Australia where we worked on HMS *Falmouth* a Type-12 frigate, staying in the barracks on Garden Island, a naval base cut out of the bush and joined to the mainland by a long bridge.

The conditions on Garden Island were excellent and the food was better than I ever had in the RN. Small wallabies called Tamars were running around the establishment as were all manner of other fauna. We were introduced to the junior sailors' bar and had many a happy evening singing songs and quaffing large quantities of ale. It was the first time I had ever had a cabin to myself in a new accommodation block; I was really impressed by the Australian Navy. The workshops were full of pristine equipment never before used. The only problem with the place was the large quantity of spiders, never my most favourite of animals at the best of times, but these were big by any standards. Looking up from your beer you would see these things hanging above you, I could have sworn that some of them had tattoos. The Australians would laugh at us as we would dive for cover. I was told these spiders were completely harmless. I decided to conquer my fear and befriend the small spider with the red backside in my cabin, the theory being that if I started with the small ones I could work up to the big ones. My Aussie chum in the next cabin entered my cabin as I was playing with Harry and to my surprise immediately squashed him. Harry it turns out was not so benign as he looked being some kind of deadly murderer according to my Aussie mate.

We spent two weeks before flying to Sydney, which I did not enjoy as much as Perth, and stayed in HMAS *Kuttabul*, the Australian Navy's barracks in Woolamaloo, right next to Kings Cross, the most notorious part of Sydney. Returning from a pub called the Chevron I was accosted by a man demanding money, I ignored him, he attacked me and I retaliated. He was soon joined by two of his associates wielding wooden sticks. I woke up in Darlinghurst general hospital with what I later found out was a broken jaw. The next three days were extremely painful. A nurse told me that it had probably been off duty policemen 'earning a few extra dollars': such a charming place. An Australian sailor keen to present a better image of his country showed me around the area in his car. We crossed Sydney Harbour Bridge and headed out into the countryside to a wildlife park where koala bears, red kangaroos, emus and wombats were kept in very good and spacious conditions. After that we went to the Returned Serviceman's League club for a few beers.

We were working on HMS *Norfolk*, a County class guided missile destroyer in Sydney; planned maintenance and a few defects kept us busy for 2 weeks before we flew home. At Sydney Airport we were charged A$10 departure tax; there were about fifty of us with not one cent between us. As we were flying on an RAF VC 10 there was no reason to expect to be charged as we had been staying in Australian government accommodation. Needless to say, rather than have fifty sailors hanging around in the airport with no money we were allowed onto the plane. This was precisely the kind of poor organisation we had become used to.

When I returned to the UK, flying via Colombo and Bahrain, my wife looked forward to me having some time at home, working in the dockyard and coming home at night. During this time I became better at my job. Working on a wide range of vessels I would pick up a job card in the base, pick up my tools, find the ship do the job and return. I liked working by myself, sometimes two of us would go along and we were fairly steaming through the work. This had a detrimental effect on my desire for promotion, because there was no one in authority who could evaluate what I had or had not done. Sometimes I would work on two or three ships a day and there was never, to my knowledge, a problem with my work. But it was very hard for my superiors to keep up with what I was doing.

In September 1979 we flew from Gatwick to Gibraltar to work on HM Ships *Hecate* (a survey vessel), *Intrepid* (Assault Ship) and *Bulwark*, an old Commando carrier known affectionately as the Rusty B. We stayed in the Montarik Hotel where three beds had been pushed into a one-bed room for two weeks, then stayed the last week on the *Bulwark*. It was here that I met Charles, a famous name in the RN, and Lottie who owned bars in Gib. Charles who owned the Hole in the Wall club was overtly homosexual and one of the funniest humans I have ever met. At the time he had a dog, a Golden Retriever called Prince. Prince would start walking up the stairs and Charles would shout 'Prince, ladies first' whereupon the dog would walk back down allowing Charles to go first. Lottie was an old lady who owned Lottie's Beer Keller on Main Street. She came from Lithuania, had married a Royal Marine and they ended up in Gib. She would play cribbage with all the sailors, invariably for money, which they would then lose. She took a torrent of abuse and when she got upset would order 'Lottie say, you just left'. I never heard of anyone arguing with this diminutive old lady.

I liked Gibraltar, for a small place it was packed with things to do. A top of the Rock race was organised, for 2½ miles from the dockyard, my legs would pump up and down and such was the incline that you felt you were standing still. I managed it in 29 minutes and still have the certificate; at that time the record was 15. I watched the apes steal the tourists' cameras, visited the Trafalgar graves, went to sea canoeing at the weekend and toured the caves.

Back at home I renewed my quest for promotion, some idiot had even written in a report that I was shy and reserved which gave my colleagues a right good laugh. I was given a chance, as normally the leading hands leadership course was completed after promotion, but I was allowed to take this two-week course whilst still a Mechanic First Class which roughly equated to Able Seaman. On my son David's first birthday I left Gosport for Chatham firmly resolved to pass the course, which was packed with things to do and was one of the most worthwhile courses I ever did in the RN. Assault courses, a two day exercise in Ashdown forest, spot lectures where you were given a subject to talk on, prepared lectures, practical leadership tasks involving getting large items across a gymnasium without touching the deck and a raft exercise across a lake were only some of the things we did. Some people pay a lot of money to send executives on such courses. The two weeks flew by and I passed the course. At the end I distributed song sheets to the class and we sang a song I had written to the course instructor, making disparaging comments on various instructors. I returned to MFMG with a good report.

What a year 1980 was. I teemed up with Bomber who though I didn't know it was to be my 'oppo' for the next four years as we constantly met up. In May the call went out to attend HMS *Juno*, a Leander class frigate currently in Haakonsvern naval base Norway. We stayed in a hotel near Bergen with so much work to do that our stay had to be extended to over a month. The poor old *Juno* had a few problems a gay scandal had resulted in a few members of the ship's company being dismissed the service and so morale was very low. Added to their problems we had arrived living in a hotel with extra money. I found them extremely resilient if a little fed up.

An American guided missile destroyer caught fire astern of the *Juno*. The Yanks asked for assistance and a grumbling party of stokers led by a Petty Officer strolled up the jetty, put out the fire and strolled back while the astonished Americans who aware of the weaponry they had on board, had been busy evacuating the ship. On another occasion a vicar and tarts' party was held on the flight deck of the *Juno*; all the crew came dressed in female attire no doubt purloined from various bedrooms around the world. The enduring image I have is of a Leading Stoker dressed in basque and stockings, holding a can of beer, looking at the Dutch frigate berthed next to the *Juno* and the long haired sailors it contained and shouting, 'Look at them long-haired poofs.' It would be amusing to discover what our allies in NATO had to say about the *Juno*.

At the weekend I travelled up the Hardanger Fjord from Ulvik to Norheimesund, then to Voss and back to Bergen with a stoker, Hoss Cartwright. It was an extremely beautiful place with waterfalls flowing from the top of huge mountains to the woody slopes below. Small houses clung to the side of the fjords and I have often wondered what it would be like to live in such a place. This was summer, in the next three years I would take part in NATO exercises in winter, my enthusiasm for the place somewhat diminished. In recent years Norway has crept back into my good books. The time flew and soon we were heading back to the Norwegian airfield where we had landed on in an RAF Hercules C130 transport. Arriving at RAF Lynham the Chief was waiting for us and informed us that we had better go home, say hello to our wives and get ready to go to Hong Kong.

Hong Kong is the most interesting of places if not the cleanest on earth; we stayed in the Singapore Hotel in Wanchai and worked on HMS *Coventry*, a Type-42 destroyer, for three weeks. The heat was terrible and by consent we opted to work at night, leaving the days free for sightseeing. We asked the boss if we could work extra hours and put it to him that if we managed to clear the outstanding work could we have some time off.

I remember taking a ferry to Lantau, an island off Hong Kong. The sights and smells of Silvermine Bay are an education in themselves. A bus took us up into the hills where we stood in the middle of nowhere, in ten minutes another bus came and we alighted at the gates of a Buddhist monastery. It was the most tranquil of places, silent monks walking around us as we inspected the finely detailed artwork. One gold statue looked incredibly lifelike. I read that when he died the monks had encased the man's body in gold. The gardens were beautiful with huge butterflies of various colours and a huge frog startled us by jumping out of an ornamental pond where large fish lazed in the sun. I looked up to the mountains that towered above the monastery and thought it was the most idyllic sight I had ever seen; it was with great reluctance that Mick Hollis and I dragged ourselves away. On the way back a local informed us that the fortified construction we were passing was the local prison and I could not help thinking that this place with all of its beauty would be a living hell as a prison; I saw no windows.

Some people did not venture out of Wanchai but Mick and I got out at every opportunity. We booked ourselves on to an all-day junk trip to an island I have forgotten the name of. A colourful spectacle of dancers and a parade worthy of Bourbon Street during the Mardi Gras awaited us. We were sure that we had stumbled upon a local festival, but it turned out to be a funeral. We followed the wrapped body to a fishing boat where it was encased in ice to be taken to who knows where for eternal rest. One enduring image I have of Hong Kong was an old ragged woman being thrown down the steps of the Hong Kong & Shanghai Banking Corporation where I was getting cash. There was a lot of poverty in Hong Kong, one man we passed regularly on our way to the dockyard lay on a bed covered in scars. At night the rats would chew his legs. I also saw whole families living in large unused drainage pipes. There was a lot of money in Hong Kong but this made no difference to the lives of those people. We also visited a Sung dynasty village; they were the first recorded society who used paper money. This was a well-constructed, mainly wooden structure which, on my last visit in 1997 I was told had been pulled down to make way for more high-rise office blocks; such is progress.

Leaving MFMG in August 1980 I went back to HMS *Collingwood* for my Leading Rates' Qualifying course. This covered electronics, electro-technology, explosive safety, management, measurements, hydraulics, control engineering and NGT or Naval General Training, covering discipline and parade ground training which in my opinion was a waste of time on a technical course. From 1980 to 1989 my only forays onto the parade ground were made in being taught how to do it. After finishing the course I learned that I had passed all the different modules including the three days spent on the 6-inch gun (which I never saw as it was only carried on one ship at the time, that was paid off that year) and due to having already passing the leadership course was rated LMEM (L). Whilst waiting for a ship I spent some time working for computer and mathematics in Collingwood, an agreeable position and the first position which involved the use of a typewriter.

In March 1981 I was told to report to Middle Dock, South Shields and join HMS *Fearless* then in dry dock.

CHAPTER IV

Fearless and the Falklands, 1981–83

HMS FEARLESS IS AN ASSAULT SHIP or LPD, an American designation meaning Landing Platform Dock. With a ballasting system the ship can lower herself in the water, open her stern door and landing craft can sail in and out of the dock taking vehicles such as tanks ashore in a landing. Her main propulsion is two steam turbines with a service speed of about 19 knots. There are four landing craft or LCU's carried on the ship which can carry a tank, and four smaller LCVP's carried on davits on the port and starboard sides. The armament carried is anti-aircraft orientated with four quadruple Seacat missile launchers and two 40mm Bofors guns on the port and starboard bridge wings. The Seacat was an elderly short-range weapon, which should in my opinion have been replaced with something like the then new Seawolf, but with defence cuts imminent this was unlikely to happen. A ramp from the vehicle deck connects with the flight deck via a door but the absence of a hangar was a serious omission. She was built by Harland and Wolf in Belfast in 1966 and at fifteen was showing her age.

I joined *Fearless* on 10/3/1981 and soon found that I was amongst friends. We settled down to the first commercial dry dock any of us had encountered. In the dock next to us was a Russian ship that stayed for several months although the Cold War was still very much alive. As we were to remain in dry dock for some time we had to find accommodation ashore. It was a blessing that the whole ship's complement of 640 were not there as there would have been a serious shortage of accommodation, especially when HMS *Euraylus* docked next door. Whilst in Middle Docks we worked out of an old warehouse and it was here I had my first real encounter with the Royal Marines. There was only a handful of them, their Corporal Smith was affectionately known as UG UG due to his caveman qualities and immense proportions. The Royal Marine motto Per Mare Per Terrum (by land, by sea) was followed by 'Perhaps' on their office door, a comment on the time already spent in South Shields. UG UG had an annoying habit of throwing darts at people coming through the door, on entering the building the hat on the side of my bag was pierced by a dart and my first meeting was decidedly heated. However you could not ignore the infectious toothless grin and UG UG soon became a friend of mine. The wife of this 6 foot 7 inch giant was extremely petite at about 5 foot. I remember at one ship's company dance they danced cheek to cheek with her feet dangling in mid-air 18 inches above the floor. Bomber had also been drafted to *Fearless* and soon the team on the ship became very close.

Sharing a terraced house in Tyne dock with four Leading Stokers was an experience never to be forgotten. On one occasion we returned home to find a cooked dinner on the table and clean windows together with a note saying would we please keep the place in better order. I do not know to this day who left the note. We were of course cooking for ourselves and did not always buy the right things. We never ran out of beer though. A new chap asked if we could put him up, which we did. Clive was an odd fellow, older than us with a Land Rover. He inquired as to whether we liked venison. One Sunday evening Clive's Landy arrived with a pair of antlers sticking out of the back. We helped him bring the deer into the house and then were struck by the question, 'What do we do now?' It had to be hung; we had an outside toilet, so up it went hanging on the cistern. Unfortunately it was the only toilet we had, no one had thought to tell one of the lad's girlfriends and off she went to the toilet. It was dark, there was no light and she went in. At this time someone remembered the deer, her screams were followed by language best not reported whilst we could not move for laughing. The word soon got around and visitors would refuse to use the lavatory. I came home late one night to find a party in full swing. I retired to have a bath and was shocked to find four females squatting on the bath side shouting at me to go away, and who did I think I was interrupting their conversation. The whole set up was extremely bizarre. We had so much venison to eat we were sick of it, breakfast dinner and tea, roast, stewed, cold, fried, pied and sautéed.

We had a great time in South Shields which was marred somewhat when a fight developed in a local night club which left several of us damaged. I ended up with a fractured cheekbone and broken nose. The young sailors joined en masse and we had to account for all of them. The idea was to muster everyone at action stations then as section leaders we would take their names. One idiot who shall remain nameless had changed his name by deed poll two weeks previously and did not let on, leaving us to comb the ship looking for his other self. We went to Portland, drills followed drills and exercises dragged on into December 1981. Having had so many on the *Bristol* I was getting weary; six months later I was glad of them.

As we entered Portsmouth I saw the *Santissima Trinidad*, an Argentinian Type-42 destroyer. As I walked through the dockyard on my way to the Isle of Wight ferry (I had bought a house in Cowes) I walked past it and commented to a friend of mine how odd it was that they were 8,000 miles from home at Christmas. Unlike most of my 'oppo's' I had a wide knowledge of naval history and an interest in politics and the trouble Jim Callaghan had had in 1979 with the Argentine Navy under Admiral Anaya who was all for taking the Falkland Islands. I have often thought since how was it that no one else could see that the Argentines were deliberately looking around Portsmouth dockyard noting the many ships in mothballs in various states of readiness and repair as the Navy was being constricted by a decreasing amount of resources. Small aircraft carriers and a limited number of assault ships would mean that, to any strategist the Royal Navy was incapable of mounting an assault to retake the Falklands should it be invaded. *Intrepid* was in the process of being retired, *Invincible* was to be sold and *Fearless* was to go to the Caribbean as a part of the Dartford Training Squadron. The arguments in Buenos Aires must have concentrated on our NATO commitments, anti-submarine and the resupply of troops in Norway being the only contribution that the Navy could be used for. The main concern was in Germany for the RAF and Army; the Navy was to be sidelined.

So off we went on a sunlit cruise, or so we thought. The two helicopters were stowed on deck due to the lack of a hangar. It was January in the North Atlantic and we hit the most awful weather that I have ever seen. Standing on the bridge I saw a wave high above us, we climbed steadily up its side for what seemed like an eternity before crashing down the other side injuring a Petty Officer cook who was thrown into an oven. The helicopters, after three days of bad weather, were wrecked and various damage was sustained around the ship.

We eventually arrived in San Juan, Puerto Rico, not my most favourite of places although we were welcomed in Fort Buchanan, the American Army base. As before I was astounded by the facilities that American servicemen enjoyed. We were poor relations constantly being told of our superiority but a quick look around an American base will soon tell you who is appreciated more, irrespective of performance.

We set sail for Port of Spain in Trinidad where I volunteered to work in the flooded-out seamen's mission. We were rewarded by being taken to a beach by Wimpey who treated us to a free bus ride and beer at the beach. We all had a great time and it was a welcome break from life on the ship. I was Leading Hand of the mess; the First Lieutenant did rounds and always insisted we clean the deck again. On the last occasion I ordered my chaps to leave the deck as it was, the officer came back and remarked on the improvement, my naivety was wearing away and I played the Navy at its own tedious game.

A moment of sadness in Trinidad happened when some locals boarded a yacht and murdered two men, their wives escaping by jumping over the side. A party from *Fearless* cleaned the mess and the yacht was put in a landing craft and later transferred to the RFA *Stromness*, which took it home. Aruba and Curacao followed; owned by the Netherlands, the Islands are pleasant but flat and not as interesting as other islands in the Caribbean. We took on Dutch marines and landed them in an exercise, which resulted in serious damage to one of our landing craft, which had grounded on a coral reef. Our last port of call was St Vincent in the Grenadines where I volunteered to work in the hospital. Without going in to too much detail I was shocked by the waste of money donated by Christian Aid. The locals were not trained to use equipment like an incinerator and other donated technical devices many of which we had to repair due to having been seriously misused. There is no doubt in my mind that after we left all devices repaired would once again be broken through ill use.

On the trip home Bomber and myself both sat our Provisional Professional Examination written and oral for Petty Officer. My oral exam seemed to last forever with our Marine Engineering Officer Commander McGregor and Fleet Chief John Price our Electrical boss. I was sent outside while they discussed my fate, was recalled and to my surprise passed, as did Bomber. As I had only been a Leading Hand for a year I had to wait another year to be promoted, but my pay increased, as I became Leading Rate scale A.

We picked up soldiers in Plymouth and proceeded to Norway to go on exercise. In a snowstorm one evening I was ordered to rig up lighting with my duty watch to 'make the ship resemble the lines of a merchant ship'. Due to visibility this was completely pointless but orders are orders. At 2000 hrs I was ordered to remove the aforementioned lights; I volunteered to switch them off but was told they had to be removed, which took forty minutes in the dark. I was furious when reporting the completion of this pointless exercise but was told to get them rigged again. I invited the young Lieutenant concerned to personally tell my now cold and tired duty watch himself. The order was cancelled. We went ashore in Harstad, a cheerless, snow-covered place with extremely expensive beer.

We came back to Portsmouth at the end of March 1982 expecting some Easter leave. At one point our Captain, E. S. J. Larken, called us on to the flight deck to tell us that the Navy was changing, some of us would lose our jobs, ships would be taken out of service. For the first time I started to consider my future as being separate from that of the Navy.

Less than a week later General Galtieri invaded, first South Georgia then the Falklands. The Government through complacency and a know-all attitude prevalent in the Foreign Office had completely misread Argentine intentions. My mind wandered back to December and the Argentinian destroyer.

All hell broke loose. I was the Leading Hand for the Outside Machinery section and we suddenly found ourselves hard at work making sure everything was up to scratch. Stores appeared, we loaded by every conceivable method, using our deck cranes, shore cranes and a hand-to-hand chain of men passing stores up the gangways. Extra ship's-company were sent to the ship and men taken from the Royal Naval Detention Quarters in the dockyard carried out a lot of the storing. Food, ammunition, fuel for the ship and the eight landing craft and ship's boats, aviation fuel for our helicopters and spare parts for all eventualities. We would of course replenish at sea from RFA's and various Merchant tankers in the course of the next 100 days but the recently completed Caribbean trip followed by a Norwegian exercise and the possibility that we were to be taken out of service had left us short on most items.

We sailed down to Ascension Island and waited for the *Intrepid* our sister ship, which had been completely de-stored and had very few crew.

Sailors were recalled from all over the country: without them it is doubtful that the islands could have been retaken. As I write this the *Fearless* is still at sea and the *Intrepid* is in mothballs with a replacement due out in 2003 – so much for lessons learnt.

The number of ships at Ascension grew to monumental proportions; I had certainly never seen so many ships in one place. Merchant vessels from several different companies and various types sat in the sun at anchor. We fished, rods appeared from everywhere, we caught sharks which were put on the menu, and little black parrot fish which resembled sea-going piranhas in looks and habit. They were so tough that they could not even be used as bait, the other fish avoided them. One of the problems we faced was disposal of garbage. It piled high on the decks and was stowed in every conceivable location. The smell and flies soon became a menace and we were anxious to get to sea.

Whilst attending the motor tug *Irishman*, which had suffered a galley fire, I had an accident falling 15 feet into a boat onto my back. I had to give directions to my mechanic to complete the job as I could barely move for the pain. On returning to the ship I was laid up for a few days, and this time was spent making up dog tags for the Electrical Department. An addition to my mess deck occurred when a young stoker refused to do what he was told, he arrived in the mess and told everyone how good he was. I left the mess deck and on returning he was considerably quieter, the chaps had had a word. I was often asked if this young man had cause to give trouble but apart from finding him lacking in social graces and ignorant beyond redemption he was otherwise manageable. At the end of the war we were awash with dextrose tablets for energy. He ate them like sweets by the handful, one wag in the mess told him they were poisonous and he would die in half an hour. He was advised to go to the sick bay and he ran towards the door. I ordered him to return to dress properly as he only had a towel around his waist. The man, with twenty-nine minutes to live, came back to put his clothes on. It was not long before the sport of baiting this skinheaded yob became boring.

The long haul south began. A lot of books have been written on the subject and with newspapermen appearing like a rash all over the ship it was totally unlike previous wars. It was not, in my opinion, advantageous to have them on the ship from an operational point of view. In contrast the Chinese laundry men who stayed were actually extremely useful. Other civilians carried were the NAAFI staff who, for the duration, donned naval uniform and operated under naval discipline.

As we sailed south in convoy the ship started going round in circles and I was asked why this was as it was extremely embarrassing. A split pin had fallen out of the feedback transmitter in the steering gear compartment which took two minutes to repair but we could have had a collision; the smallest of items can result in the loss of a ship. During a replenishment at sea the sky took on a coppery hue. I have never seen a sky like it as the light appeared to be lost in the clouds and I looked upon the scene of sailors running around the deck pulling ropes and moving hoses and boxes with a kind of surreal fascination.

The war got hotter, HMSm *Conqueror* torpedoed and sunk the *General Belgrano*, HMS *Sheffield* was bombed by the Argentineans and sunk. I do not remember anyone thinking that this was totally unexpected; in my mess we always knew that there were going to be losses. The decision to sink *Belgrano* was a correct one; she was armed with Exocets and heavy guns and was a threat. I have heard many times that she was turning away, but as anyone who has studied naval battles and manoeuvres knows this is misleading. At the battle of North Cape in 1943 the *Scharnhorst* veered off on more than one occasion in an effort to reappear closer to a protective convoy. It takes no time at all to turn a ship. Another outcome of the sinking of the *Belgrano* was the defeat of the Argentine Navy by keeping it in port nervous of submarine attack. The biggest issue was the reluctance of the Argentine aircraft carrier *Vincentino De Mayo* to sail; to those of us on vulnerable, reasonably slow landing ships this was a welcome omission. Most of the news took time to filter to us and I would not be surprised if people at home knew about the operation before we did. I found that to have my mail censored by the Padre, when it was only going to my wife, was extremely offensive when organisations like the BBC regularly blurted out information that could have been used to adverse effect, with life-threatening consequences.

We took troops from the *Canberra* on the 19 May 1982 and on the 20th entered San Carlos Water behind a Type-21 frigate. There was always a risk of mines and as I sat at my action station my mind began to wander – what would it be like to hit a mine or take a bomb. Would I see it come through the side of the ship, or would I just not know? In the next month a large number of people would find out the hard way.

I have no idea how long I spent at my action station during the war. I was part of 3.2 damage control section base, my task being to supply electrical power to equipment should the cables be damaged. In this part of the ship we had the ballast control room and access to the dock. One landing craft had to be pumped out on returning to *Fearless* and we had to rig up a submersible pump to pump it out. We had very little air cover; bombing raids were sometimes forecast but on too many occasions we had little or no warning. The only two ships carrying aircraft capable of air-to-air combat were far to the east. One later landed on *Fearless* to refuel; this only happened once and because the aircraft had to land vertically a lot of fuel was used. Whilst not wishing to denigrate the efforts of either ship or the pilots of the few hard-pressed Harriers it was woefully inadequate air cover. The Argentinean Navy suffered the loss of a submarine (the *Santa Fe*), a cruiser (*General Belgrano*) and various small commercial vessels like the trawler *Narwhal*. The capture of the *Yehuin*, an old offshore supply vessel, will be dealt with in a later chapter. The RN on the other hand was hammered by the Argentine Air Force. Two Type-42 destroyers, *Sheffield* and *Coventry*, two Type-21 frigates *Ardent* and *Antelope*, and the *Atlantic Conveyor*, a large container vessel, were sunk by Argentine aircraft LSL RFA *Sir Galahad* had to be taken out and sunk it was so badly damaged, *Sir Tristram* only narrowly avoiding the same fate but was put out of action for a long time afterwards. Then there were ships that were hit but still operational, HMS *Plymouth*, HMS *Glasgow*, HMS *Antrim*, HMS *Andromeda*, RFA *Sir Lancelot* and one of our Landing Craft F4.

We flew out to several ships for the purposes of damage repair and fire fighting from *Fearless*. I found myself helicoptered to the badly damaged *Sir Tristram* to restore electrical power, which we somehow managed. The emergency switchboard was very badly damaged, and we worked at cutting away the damaged parts. At the end I looked at the MEA who had been checking out the engine, there was a silent moment between us, then I pushed the start button and instinctively ducked. The generator burst into life, what a beautiful sound.

The Argentinians had driven sheep into the water and dead sheep floated, legs up, everywhere. I have no idea why they did this and it confirmed their unsuitability to govern the Falklands. The RFA *Sir Galahad* smoked in the distance, *Tristram* looked bad enough; it was a grim reminder of what could so easily have happened to our own ship.

FEARLESS AND THE FALKLANDS, 1981–83

*RFA Sir Tristram in Bluff Cove 1982.
Showing the exit hole of the bomb.*

Due to the losses incurred, the financial burden that the taxpayer has had to endure ever since the Falklands has been immense. The mine clearance alone being a never-ending task has resulted in the maiming of servicemen long after the war. The short-sighted attitude taken by all political parties which has left the armed forces in poor condition for successive generations is hard to understand. It is significant that in the Second World War Great Britain, which had complied with treaties on arms while others did not, was unprepared. In 1982 Margaret Thatcher could only ask if the armed forces could retake the Falklands; those in charge had no choice but to say yes even though they had doubts. Despite developing the aircraft carrier, we had not even reached the internationally agreed ceiling in 1939; the admirals thought it was not needed, the significance of its role being underestimated. So our losses in the Second World War to aircraft were heavy, our carriers small, and the aircraft slow and obsolete. This attitude is endemic in British high command

Me and my mechanic. Me on the left, Keith Hallas on the right. Damage to the bridge extensive

and government; perhaps in future if we are not going to do it properly we should just not bother. We had Harriers in the Falklands; too few to stop the air raids. Harriers were hampered by their low top speed in relation to the opposition. American-supplied missiles worked, our own Sea Dart and Rapier, in which the British public had invested large amounts of money, were not as effective as expected. Sea Cat scared us more than the enemy and a look on the barrels on our Bofors confirmed that the most effective anti-aircraft weapon on the *Fearless* was of Second World War vintage.

Most of my time was spent at my action station; at night I manned one of the electrical switchboards, doubling up as an on-call crane driver. During the war I lifted rotor stacks into helicopters, a captured anti-aircraft gun onto a trawler and various boats for various operations. It was impossible to sleep in San Carlos as charges were dropped from boats every 10 minutes to deter divers. Washing also became a rarity; I never seemed to get time. At the end this became more pronounced, as we had to fly here and there to attend ships that had been hit.

During action I had to repair damage to instruments on the bridge wings caused by 40mm cartridges flying everywhere. We also sustained damage from aircraft cannon but thankfully it was light. There were some injuries to a Bofors gun crew with one young lad being badly disabled. Damage from overuse of equipment took most of our time and I found myself on the end of a safety harness trying to repair the connection box for the helicopter start rectifier. With an air raid ever imminent that was the fastest repair I have ever carried out. With the enemy aircraft flying so low, there was always the possibility that you would be hit by fire from enthusiastic troops ashore.

The landing craft F4 was hit by bombs killing 6 of our ship's company 2 sailors and 4 Royal Marines including Colour Sergeant Johnson. The sailors were MEA James and LMEM (M) Miller who I knew very well. I had been told that Phil Thickett, another Leading Electrician, had been on board and was pleasantly surprised to see him walking along the port alleyway. With all of the losses being due to aircraft attack it would be easy to blame the command at the time but they could only use what they had. It would also be easy to blame John Nott, the Minister for Defence. In truth it was the result of a muddle, a declining empire with a lot of responsibilities overseas, the need to divert funds to public services and tax cuts. The government of the time was faced with many conflicting interests, not least of which was our responsibility to protect the Falkland Island people from a harsh right wing regime who thought nothing of 'disappearing' their own people. My mind went back to the debate on Gibraltar; again a Fascist government given to murdering its own people had ruled for some years in Spain. I have no doubt that the decision to retake the Falklands was correct; the arrogance of the Foreign Office and the constant demands for cuts from the treasury are another matter.

On leaving a RN ship or establishment it is necessary to fill in a drafting preference card to tell the drafting officer if you had a preference for your next draft. After *Bristol* I had entered 'Type-42 destroyer based Portsmouth'; after the Falklands I changed it to, 'Fishery protection vessel based Rosyth'. Building ships out of a metal which catches fire at a lower temperature was never the best of ideas. If Naval Architects had been required to sail and fight in the vessels they designed, coping with their problems, it would be doubtful if some of the Navy's poorer designs

Bahia Pariso. Argentine Red Cross ship suspected of supplying ammunition

would have ever got off the ground. It was noticeable by the damage on *Tristram*, which had no bridge or accommodation left, but a virtually undamaged hull, that something was wrong. It was only in later years that I learnt that the metal of the accommodation and bridge were similar to the hulls of later designs whilst the hull was built in a traditional way. Whilst flying over the Falklands I photographed the Argentine ship *Bahia Paraiso* a so-called Red Cross vessel. This ship was suspected of supplying arms, especially Exocets, to the troops.

In June the Argentinians collapsed, we had won but it had been too close for comfort. We had been extremely lucky not to be hit by a bomb, and we had our fair share of near misses; if they exploded the shock wave would hit the ship with a sound similar to the hull being hit with a hammer. Our now depleted stores were being used by prisoners of war that had been billeted on the now empty vehicle decks. Whilst repairing some bridge instruments in San Carlos I required a resistor and various electronic components. The instruments had been damaged by cartridges ejecting from the Bofors 40mm AA gun. A bag was fitted to catch them but so many had been fired that the bag could not cope. A Stores Assistant informed me that the stores were emergency only and not to be used. A heated argument ensued and I eventually had to rely on higher authority. I received the spare parts eventually and asked the dimwit in stores what could be more of an emergency than a warship in action expecting an air raid at any minute with damaged equipment that the Captain deemed necessary. This attitude was prevalent in Naval Stores, both uniform and civilian, and I never understood it. Having said that, in general the Falklands were won on logistics and it was inevitable that mistakes would be made.

The efforts of the Merchant Navy were without doubt a major reason for our success. I later joined a Merchant vessel that belonged to a merchant shipping company, which had supplied vessels with British officers and crew to the government. One such vessel, the Motor Tanker *Scottish Eagle*, had spent two years in the Falklands with men having 'volunteered' for service. In fact they had been told that if they did not volunteer the company might not be able to employ them in the future. When the ship finally returned to Southampton they were met by the personnel manager and everyone was sacked. A few weeks later some of the officers were offered positions in a new company, actually the same company with the same office in London. Those that returned did so on reduced terms with untrained Bangladeshi crew. This turned out to be the first company that I worked for when I left the Navy in 1989. British merchant seaman are extremely resilient, working as we do for some of the most ruthless and cut-throat companies in existence.

In July 1982 we returned to Portsmouth, John Nott came on board and I remember feeling hostile on meeting him. He actually smiled at me and I had an almost uncontrollable urge to kick him senseless. Luckily our Captain, who I respected, was there showing him round ... I put on my uniform and lined up on the deck to see thousands of people cheering and waving as we entered Portsmouth, boats hooted, the noise was incredible. At the time I wondered what they were all so happy about. As we came around the newly completed HMS *Liverpool* to Fountain Lake Jetty I struggled to see if my wife was there. She was only two weeks away from having our second son, Michael James Nicholas. She was with David, her mum Jean and dad Bill, and I was relieved to see them. My own parents could not make it as Dad was at Coulport RNAD. One of the torpedoes he had looked after, as Services Engineer, had been the undoing of *Belgrano*.

We put the ship on shore electrical supply and I went home to the Isle of Wight for the night, returning the next day. My house was completely covered in flags and bunting, I was overawed.

At a very early hour on 2 August 1982 I witnessed the birth of Michael; my wife still complains that I got more attention from the nurses than she did. I took some leave; we had a christening, which was preceded by a jolly night out in Cowes, which ended in a lamppost-climbing contest admirably won by my father-in-law.

The ship dry-docked in Portsmouth and underwent a lot of repairs, primarily to the steering gear, which had always been prone to leaks. After the docking we exercised off Ejsberg with NATO. The American assault ships were so much more versatile than ours and bigger. After this we reverted to our role of Dartmouth Training Squadron, taking young officers on jollies around sunny climes. On this occasion it was to be the Mediterranean and not the wisest of choices for the RN due to there being uninformed sympathy for the Argentine cause, especially in Italy and Greece. Further problems were caused when we later called at Brest.

Another problem was that due to trickle drafting, which ensures that the crew is constantly changing, the bonds between the members of *Fearless* ship's company who had been in action in the Falklands were so strong that newcomers were looked upon as intruders. This is not a reflection on them, but rather on ourselves and the way we had changed. One chap had served on *Coventry* and after abandoning ship and embarking in a lifeboat, had dived back into the freezing South Atlantic to rescue another sailor, but his experiences belonged to him and *Coventry* not us and *Fearless*.

The first port was Gibraltar. I had the duty of shore patrol in the afternoon and early evening. Despite one incident (which was defused) I had a quiet patrol. That night a significant number of the ship's company were arrested and this was to set the tone for the rest of that most unfortunate trip. Naples was next, the Italian Navy took us to Pompeii and a Cameo factory, visits I enjoyed. Then the American Navy entered port and the mood changed. One particular instance involved a diminutive mechanic from Hartlepool getting bored with all the talk and bravado of the Americans. He made disparaging remarks about their attempt to release hostages in Iran and losing several helicopters on the way. The result of that remark is best left unrecorded.

After Naples came Split in the former Yugoslavia. As it was a communist country we all had to go ashore in uniform, a target may as well have been painted on us; taunts about the loss of the *Sheffield* provoked more trouble. As I was keen on running I took part in an organised 7-mile run which took us over the hills around the town, which I found to be an extremely pleasant and photogenic place. Not content with this we next found ourselves in Salonika in Greece. On occasion we would be spat at when ashore and it was here that I fractured the metacarpals in my left hand. After one fracas we met a Greek called Simon who owned a bar. He knew when he was onto a good thing and we soon organised a football match, which we lost to Simon's team. I was in goal and the swamp behind me was home to the greatest amount of mosquitoes that I have ever seen; they were huge and my excuse is that I was diverted from my task. The Greeks seemed immune to these monsters whilst I was covered in bites.

Istanbul followed Greece and an interlude from trouble; we toured a Turkish brewery which to my surprise was modern and clean. However most of Istanbul was dirty and backward. It would be interesting indeed for a Canadian female friend of ours, who has on occasion told me how wonderful the Islamic religion is, to see how well she would cope with living in Turkey on a full-time basis. A party in the British Consulate ended up in a food fight and certain members of the ship's company had to clean it up the next day. The bazaar was interesting and I developed a taste for the gritty coffee served in the cafés. I have been back many times but it is an unseemly place and I no longer venture ashore. From Istanbul we departed for Venice with which I was fascinated, again no trouble and I was beginning to think we had left all of that behind us.

The final port was Brest. Trouble flared when the ship's company were taunted about the achievement of French Exocet missiles. I tried to stay out of trouble; my only recollection was that I had to pay towards the cost of replacement of a plate-glass shop front through which an unfortunate Frenchmen had been thrown. It was not a happy trip and it was with some relief that we arrived in Portsmouth for Christmas. A ship's magazine called the *Showboat* had been brought out at the instigation of Commander Kelly, the Executive Officer. This was never popular on the lower deck, as we always felt that it trivialised the ship's achievements. In retrospect we should have welcomed the mood, but the happiness we were accustomed to before the war never returned. We were taking ourselves too seriously, the ship's company formed into cliques made up of those who had taken part in the Falklands on *Fearless*, others who had been involved on other ships and those who had not. It was not a healthy state of affairs. By now I had spent nearly two years on her and I knew that I did not have long left on the ship.

In January 1983 we left Portsmouth for another jaunt in the Caribbean, this time stowing the helicopters in landing craft for the crossing and avoiding the damage we had sustained the year before. I remember this as an excellent trip despite one incident with a sailor who against all advice went to the Black Angus in San Juan, Puerto Rico. He was relieved of his wallet in the toilet and on returning to the ship was threatened with a gun and had to hand over his clothes; he returned to the ship in his underwear to the great delight of those on gangway duty. A mechanic called Sticky Green (sticky is a common nickname for Greens, for an explanation read *Jack Speak* by Rick Jolly) and myself went to Fort Buchanan and befriended a sergeant of the Puerto Rico Army National Guard. He took us home where his wife fed us beans and rice, the next day he was invited on the ship with his son who we entertained.

Next came another pleasant interlude in Tortola British Virgin Islands. This is a most beautiful Island; our ship's rugby team played their police in stifling heat. As for myself I relaxed at the yacht club with a large beer after an exhilarating swim. On the way back to catch the boat to the ship that was at anchor I went into a bar run by a Liverpudlian lady who made us the best rum punches we ever had.

We next called in at Pensacola navy base in Florida; it was here that I saw the kind of trouble caused by mixing different sex crews on a warship. The USS *Lexington* an American aircraft carrier, was having problems: the US Navy had decided to put a large number of females onboard. The first thing to happen was the wives of the men demonstrated, then the discipline started to break down. One crew member told me that he could not concentrate on what he was doing and soon affairs between ratings and officers meant that you could not trust the judgement of a love struck boss. The argument over homosexuals was a similar one and in my opinion it was pointless making homosexuality illegal once mixed-sex crews were allowed. In my mess deck we had a homosexual who had been enticing two young cooks into drinking amounts they could not cope with and then interfering with them. He was taken off the ship and charged with homosexuality that was easier to prove than indecent assault on non-consenting sixteen year olds. The same can be said for women on ships, I have no objection to an all-female crew but liberalism while sounding nice rarely deals with practicalities. The *Lexington*'s problems meant that she was no longer an efficient fighting unit, and that's dangerous. Studies by the Israeli army showed men more likely to be killed or injured in a mixed-sex regiment. It is natural for a man to try to protect a female whether she wants it or not. In fact most women stand back and let men get on with it. In our politically-correct age a few people who do not have to go into combat have made rules for those who do and that is simply unfair to everyone.

Pensacola, a naval air base, had a lot of facilities. I took part in a 12.5-mile run around the base. Due to a fire on our stern ramp hydraulics (which I took part in putting out) we had to stay a few days longer. We had three fires that trip, being in the fire party as Electro Technical Advisor I was involved in all three. Spontaneous combustion set fire to the after rope locker, a burnt-out motor caught fire on the after hydraulics and a confusing fan room fire. The smoke from the burning fan room sent smoke into a store eight decks below it. Being first on the scene I put on breathing apparatus and with very poor visibility climbed down a four-deck ladder and groped around looking for the seat of the fire. After I realised that the smoke was coming out of the ventilation I pushed the other fellow with me out of the compartment and raced up the ladder. I had been involved with the ship's ventilation and entered a fan space where a burning rubbish bag ignited by a cigarette was extinguished with a small extinguisher.

We detached four of the larger landing craft, which made their way to New Orleans independently. The Landing Craft F4, sunk in the Falklands was replaced by another which was designated FJ, in remembrance of Colour Sergeant Johnson. We followed a few days later after towing targets for the US Air force, a worrying time given that the Americans have a tendency to bomb their own. We survived witnessing probably the last rocket firing from our own Wessex helicopters.

We sailed up the Mississippi river to New Orleans and arrived in time for Mardi Gras. Bourbon Street and Royal Street were full of people, music filled the air and we had a really good time. The ship's Royal Marine band marched in one of the parades. It was breathtaking. One of my mechanics had been put on shore patrol with the New Orleans Police. After four hours he volunteered for another four-hour stretch; I never remember that happening anywhere else in my whole naval career. In a darkened bar I saw an old lady (I would estimate she was at least seventy) seemingly glide up to the bar, but the barman refused to serve her saying she had already drunk too much and he didn't want any trouble. She abused him verbally using the choicest of expressions and glided towards the door. We got up and intrigued rushed to the door to see her roller skating down the street, the barman shrugged his shoulders and told us that she did that every week.

We left New Orleans, after all the excitement it was good to get to sea. We called in to Freeport, Grand Bahama where Captain Larken rated me Petty Officer. The Captain was a remarkable man, being a nephew of Shackleton I suppose it was probably genetic. He later became an Admiral and at a reunion some years later I was surprised that he remembered me, with a normal crew of 640 with hundreds of others embarked such as aircrew, soldiers and marines this was a rare gift. Sticky carried my bags to the Petty Officers' mess 01H0, the Chinese tailor made me a new uniform and I entered another world. There were about thirty Petty Officers and this was the first mess that I shared with non-technical people. We had a bar and although there were restrictions we were no longer rationed to three cans of warm beer a day. Now we had pints of Courage Sparkling Bitter; specially brewed for the Royal Navy and RFA it can suffer fluctuations in temperature without adverse effect; it tastes good as well.

We sailed back across the Atlantic and I was to depart from the vessel in Portsmouth on 9 April 1983 for some leave before going back to HMS *Collingwood* for my Petty Officers' Qualifying course. We still had to take part in a NATO exercise in Norway but I was marking time knowing that I had come to the end of my time on what I have always considered to be the best ship I served on in the Navy.

CHAPTER V

On the Move 1983–84

I WAS CONSIDERING leaving the Navy, but I now had two children and realised that to do so would not be in the best interests of my family. The Petty Officers' technical course was on the same lines as the Leading Hands with the difference that we did not have to march to classes. The technical content was obviously more but the course was relatively short lasting from 9 May to 28 July 1983. I have never liked schoolwork but did what I had to do and duly passed the component parts of the course. All I needed was to pass the Petty Officers' Leadership Course at HMS *Royal Arthur* in Wiltshire keep the rate for a year and I would be promoted from Acting to confirmed Petty Officer.

I enjoyed the Petty Officers' Leadership Course but found it mostly irrelevant. Several times a week we would muster on the parade ground and a scratchy record of band music would be relayed through loudspeakers, which we would march to. It was pathetic and I soon became disillusioned, if things are going to be done they should be done properly. The class had to choose a leader after which to name itself – ours was Thatcher Course after the Prime Minister at the time. The Navy could not justify a band in such a small establishment but in a service full of technical knowledge the vintage record player and dodgy speakers could have been done away with; it would have made a good project for an apprentice. I did well on the physical side of the course but started taking the mickey out of the course instructors. This would be met with demands for more press-ups and points removed for various activities. We spent two days in the Black Mountains, which was very enjoyable and walked across Salisbury Plain. In the middle of the course I ran the Glasgow Marathon with my father, raising money for Cystic Fibrosis Research, in 3 hours 48 minutes. Dad came in five minutes behind me. We had friends in the Isle of Wight whose children suffered from this terrible disorder, but I felt so powerless to help. The only way I could was to raise money for the charity.

We all had to take charge of what was called a Practical Leadership Task; mine was the Internal Security Exercise. I put perimeter patrols on the outside of the camp, as I knew instructors would be posing as terrorists. All teams were armed (no bullets) and I had to control them from HQ1 by radio. I received a call from one team who had a suspect in sight, so I told them to arrest him; they promptly jumped on a very irate farmer out shooting rabbits. We were chastised but I could not help laughing, as this exercise occurred every week on the same day with different classes. In my opinion he regularly took a look at what the Navy was doing, other courses never thought of putting anyone on the outside, and he got caught out.

Another PLT took the form of a party, which my unfortunate fellow Electrician had to organise. The Commander and his wife had to be invited, the rest of the class had to help. Unfortunately a group of ladies known affectionately as F Troop gatecrashed the party helped by the class who had the party the week before who just happened to have gate duty on that day. All attempts at making sure they stayed out were thwarted; as the chap who was organising it was being assessed he was of course worried about the whole set-up. This made for an amusing interlude, but hardly tested leadership qualities.

Another part of the course involved being transported to an abandoned village, involving security, first aid, catering, getting people across a lake using ropes and tackles and with the camp staff acting as refugees. I found this to be very beneficial dealing with issues I had not thought of.

Visits by a prison governor and lectures on drugs were also illuminating. A recent film glorifying the life of a violent criminal was dealt with by the governor in a way that made me think about society in general. I passed the course and headed on to my new job on 22 September 1983 in Harbour Training Ships as an Instructor.

Between September 1983 and July 1984 I moved around a lot I was now convinced that I had to get out of the Navy but was uncertain as to what I was going to do in 'civvy street'. So I stayed and ran the course for Auxiliary Machinery Certificate Electrical Switchboards, which I largely rated as a waste of time. We had two elderly frigates, HMS *Russell* and HMS *Ashanti*, on which we had classrooms. Each course lasted one week, which I would instruct, and then mark exam papers. On one occasion I was pulled in because one young man had failed one of my exams. He had attained 22%; the pass mark was 65%, and most of the class attained on average 80%. Apparently this was my fault, so I rebelled and telephoned the establishment that drafts people around saying that I wanted a move. I asked for a fishery protection vessel based in Scotland and was told that to get it I had to join Naval Party 1242 in the Falklands as Weapons Electrical Officer of HMP *Falkland Sound*. This turned out to be Her Majesty's Prize; in fact it was the old *Yehuin*, an offshore supply vessel captured during the Falklands War. On 16 December 1983 I left HTS and headed for RAF Brize Norton to fly to Ascension Island.

We flew to Dakar in Senegal and were told to leave the plane and stay on the airfield; we were unable to go to the terminus as some soldiers had caused trouble on a former occasion. Large millipedes and lizards kept us interested for some time but the heat was terrible after coming from a UK winter. The millipedes were particularly fascinating but I couldn't eat a whole one.

At Ascension we lined up on the runway and boarded helicopters, which ferried us to the *Uganda*. She belonged to P&O and this was the first occasion that I had a cabin to myself at sea, complete with en-suite this was extreme luxury and I felt sorry for the Junior Ratings cramped in the dormitories which had been set up for school children when *Uganda* was cruising around the Med as a floating school. We soon fell into the routine on board and I remember having a wonderful time including a very good Christmas dinner. A show was arranged in the cinema. There were only six sailors, large numbers of RAF personnel and soldiers plus some civilians. There were six acts on with four coming from the Navy, two from the Army and the others refused. I always thought that the RAF acted more like civilians than the Army and Navy and put this down to the lifestyle on an RAF base, which is far more civilised than a ship, or army barracks. If I had my time again I would join the RAF but then I probably would not have been able to write so many stories. My cousin seems to spend more time skiing than in the air and has become a qualified skiing instructor, a channel not open to anyone in the Navy that I knew. On Christmas day we served 'Gunfire' to the troops in bed, that is tea liberally laced with rum. I was surprised to see how many soldiers did not want it; to me it was a sign of changing times. I am willing to bet that in 1975 that would be unusual.

We entered Port Stanley on the 30 December 1983 and I was taken by boat to join the dirtiest, most unreliable and uncomfortable vessel it has ever been my misfortune to serve on. We were part of a squadron of merchant tugs based at Navy Point, a cold and desolate place with a lot of people living in tents who had to brave icy conditions to get to a shower block with the need to traverse duckboards. It was like something from the trenches of the First World War. This was disgraceful organisation by the Royal Navy having had eighteen months to sort things out.

The other tugs belonged to a company called United Towing, and consisted of the *Irishman* (that I had worked on in 1982), the *Yorkshireman* and the *Salvageman* a large salvage tug. The Mate of the *Irishman* told me that they had refused to serve on the vessel that I was on which is why the Navy had to man it.

HMP *Falkland Sound* had been built in Germany in the mid-1960s to supply oil rigs. Originally she had been called the *Millerntor*, her design had been taken from American tugs with the two main diesel engines exhausting out of two low 'smoke stacks' aft. At least two of her sister ships had been sunk when in rough weather seawater entered the exhausts. I was told that when this happened there were usually no survivors. There was one Lieutenant who was the Captain, three Senior Rates including myself and Eleven Junior Ratings.

To list all the defects on this ship would take forever. It was very dirty, the generators were unreliable and a portable generator sat on the after deck; the gyro had been destroyed by our own soldiers when they had captured the ship and it seems that they had indulged themselves in wanton vandalism. In my time in the armed forces I found that as time progressed this was becoming more normal and was a worrying trend. To my horror I discovered that there were rats on board, large rats with thick fur. I was told that they had adapted to the harsh environment, which is why they looked bigger. At night I walked out on deck at about midnight to find out what was going on, to find several sailors chasing rats around with all manner of brooms and mops. This had to stop but to my surprise the Captain refused to acknowledge that any rats were on the ship. It was his first command and I was forbidden to report this to the Army environmental health unit, which soon became a bone of contention.

We had several jobs; one which was particularly distasteful was to pull up alongside various merchant vessels whereupon they would empty their garbage on the after deck. We would then head out to sea and dispose of it over the side to avoid polluting the harbour. We took stores to the odd settlement and boarded a couple of nosey Polish trawlers. We were well known in Port Stanley – with the cold weather and rustic washing arrangements we looked a right filthy bunch. One naval vessel we parked alongside refused to believe we were in the same navy. We had our own flag, a black pig on a yellow background; the ship was painted black and was known as the Black Pig. It seemed that we were volunteered for all kinds of duties. With the Chief Engineer, Les Batchelor, we complained about the state of the electrical system. The Navy bought a brand-new 350kW generator and parked it on the deck. I pointed out that as the deck at sea was very often covered in seawater this was likely to fail, but I was ignored.

The inevitable happened. One morning at 0500 our beloved Captain roused us and put us in one of the most dangerous situations I have encountered at sea. The weather was atrocious; the tugs had all gone out to pull merchant ships that had dragged their anchors back into position. To my surprise we were to 'help' them. We left Navy Point with our first task to get in the way of all the trained tug men who shouted abuse over the VHF only to be told to use correct voice procedure. We made a sharp turn, a wave engulfed the generator, which then blew up. This left us with no power, the engines stopped and I made my way down to the after deck. Luckily I had already told the cook to fill every container we had with water; without the electric pump we were waterless. The stator coils were blown, but Les and I managed to get another generator on and we both told the Captain to get alongside as quick as he could. We had nearly ended up on the rocks in a heavy sea, so he headed back and the generator expired just as we were tying up. I went ashore and managed to borrow a small camping generator to give us at least the ability to make a hot drink. It shows the ignorance of the Lieutenant that he asked if we could run the ship's lighting on this generator. At 16 amps this was not likely, so he was told he could either have the fire or the kettle but not both at the same time. The temperature dropped, it began to snow and we huddled together in the crew mess occasionally venturing out to check the ropes.

My idea had always been to put a smaller generator in the engine room by cutting a hole in the deck and removing one of the ship's generators, mounting the new one in its place. This would have saved a lot of problems, although of course electrical power was not our only problem. Most of the crew had submitted eighteen months notice prior to joining the vessel, we still had rats and the engine room was a disaster area prone to flooding.

The next morning Les and myself walked around the fog-bound harbour (therefore no boats) to the Army's Falkland Island logistics base to plead for a new generator. We looked like pirates, grimy, cold and fed up. The Major assured us of support and we walked back. That afternoon a mexi float, which is really a floating pontoon with an engine on the back capable of heavy lift, arrived with a crane and a new generator, which was only capable of supplying us with hotel services.

People were getting fed up, the rats still plagued us and we could get no spares. An Admiral arrived on a fact-finding mission, we were warned not to tell him anything, but only an idiot could fail to notice the conditions we were living in. I killed a rat and hung it up the mast, the tug *Irishman* which always berthed outboard of us found six in a rope locker, but still the Captain refused to get anyone in to deal with them. Visitors to the ship sympathised when they saw the state we were in. The Argentinians had left such an awful mess; I removed and scrubbed the carpet in my cabin but could not get the oil out. To walk barefoot in my cabin was to get black feet.

On a high note Jim Davidson arrived on the island and I volunteered to stay on board and let the lads go and see him; they all had a good time. We used to get invited to all kinds of parties; I was invited to the RAMC Sergeants' Mess. My leading stoker was not a senior NCO but I asked if I could bring my doggie, we had a good night and made a good-humoured assault on their bar to remove the antlers that were hanging above it. The antlers came from South Georgia where the Norwegians had released deer for food; the Norwegians were gone but the deer were still there. I tied the antlers to my head and walked back to the ship. On returning to the ship I was met by the Captain, an argument ensued and he demanded to know where the antlers had come from. I replied 'A reindeer, where do you think.' The argument continued in the galley; I had had enough.

My world changed a little bit – for the first time I had lost respect for authority, despite all efforts I was stopped by lethargy from authorities ashore, and a man who had been given a command and wanted to keep everything under wraps. It was decided I needed some rest and recuperation. I joined the RFA *Sir Percivale* and headed off to South Georgia. The *Falkland Sound* was going nowhere fast.

It was here that I met Sergeant Mick Ford who was also diagnosed as requiring R&R. South Georgia was spectacular. As we entered the harbour of Grytviken I was speechless; it is still my favourite place in the world. I climbed up the mountain and despite the cold only reluctantly came down. I visited Shackleton's grave and that of the unfortunate Argentinean submariner killed when the *Santa Fe*, which was still in the harbour at that time, was captured. Walking along the beach we saw huge elephant seals laying amongst the thousands of whalebones. Grytviken had been a Norwegian whaling station until 1966 when the Japanese took over until 1968. Now the power station, laboratory, library, houses and church were all empty. The church, built in 1913 and having withstood 70 years of Antarctic weather, had been vandalised by the British Army as had the small whalers tied up to the jetty. As you walked along the beach small fur seals charged out of the dunes; they can bite and we watched out for them. I was amazed at the penguins which just sat and took no notice of us as we wandered into their midst. There were huge piles of whalebones and harpoon heads lying around; the slaughter must have reached monumental proportions. I could have stayed in Grytviken a lot longer than I did; I have been back since but never tire of its serenity and harsh beauty.

After what had amounted to a small holiday we returned to Port Stanley. The Chief Engineer was waiting and showed me what had been done to the ship. A new 110kW generator had been put in as we had asked; no more fears of deck flooding. We later took a party up to a settlement called San Salvador about 80 miles up the coast with some dignitaries who spent most of the trip being very sick. I was relieved as planned on 16 April 1984. On the ship I was promoted to Confirmed Petty Officer, I was surprised to be recommended for promotion by the Captain. My relief looked around the ship with dismay – he was supposed to stay four months, I had been there longer.

Shortly after I left the ship the army environmental health team came on board and after finding harmful bacteria in the galley condemned the ship. She was put alongside in Port Stanley and was still there in 1989 when I last visited the island. All of our heartache as we had struggled to keep machinery running could have been avoided. Since 1982 I had had a busy time and was feeling decidedly jumpy. So much had happened on that ship it seemed as if we never stopped, disaster following disaster. A new mechanic was electrocuted when he did something I had told him not to – he was OK but it took him three days to recover. A nurse known to us all was killed when fire broke out in the hospital (she had gone back in to look for patients when an oxygen bottle exploded), the Mate from the *Irishman* was badly burnt when he was covered in battery acid and we were called to clean up after a merchant seaman had been cut in half by a parting wire. There were other incidents, which I will save for another time as I am still trying to sort out in my mind what was going on.

On 16 April 1984 I thankfully boarded an RAF Hercules C130 transport home. It took eleven hours to reach Ascension in a cramped condition because there were sick people (some on drips) in the middle of the aircraft being taken to hospitals in the UK. We transferred in Ascension to a VC10 but after flying for an hour we had to return as one of the engines had failed. We were put in tents that night, which were extremely uncomfortable in the heat especially as we had just arrived from a cold climate.

I returned home and made plans for moving to Scotland, my orders were to join Rosyth Fleet Maintenance Group for a while before being drafted to HMS *Orkney* an Island Class offshore patrol vessel.

In FMG I worked on a variety of minor vessels including HMS *Abdiel* the last purpose-built minelayer left in the Royal Navy and a variety of minesweepers of the Ton Class and mine hunters of the Hunt Class. I was briefly seconded to Flag Officer Sea Training and sailed on a minesweeper to monitor their fire drills, setting off smoke bombs to simulate fires and blacking the ship out to test the ship's staff reactions; the ship is always in a safe area when this is tested and I could not start until given permission from the command.

On 17 July 1984 I flew from Edinburgh to Thurso, then Stromness in the Orkney Islands to join HMS *Orkney* on fishery protection duties. The times were changing fast, the ship had not yet entered harbour, so I went into the Ferry Tavern at the end of the jetty and enquired about the *Orkney*. No one had ever heard of the ship despite the fact that she had been there on more than one occasion. The British public who had cheered the Royal Navy only two years previously were now no longer interested in its servicemen. As it is the people who drive the government, we can only expect damaging cuts in defence spending, until the country finds itself in a position where force is required.

ON THE MOVE 1983–84

Since the Falklands our servicemen and women have served in the Gulf, Bosnia, Northern Ireland, Belize, Sierra Leone, Kosovo and no doubt many other operations. Ignore the armed forces at your peril.

CHAPTER VI

RN – End of the Line, 1984–89

HMS ORKNEY was built in 1975 by Hall Russell of Aberdeen; she was armed with a 40mm Bofors gun, had two Ruston Paxman main engines and one shaft. I was surprised by the slow speed of this patrol vessel, which was only 16 knots. She eventually paid off from the Navy in 1999, so after twenty-four years of service the Navy got its money's worth. She was equipped with two Avon 16-foot Searider RIBs or Rigid Inflatable Boats. The boats had outboard motors and the cox'n of the boat sat on a central pillar with a steering wheel, gear and throttle levers in front of him.

On joining I was surprised to see that the Captain was Lt Cdr John Prime who had been the navigating officer on the *Fearless*. During air raids in the Falklands he had given amusing running commentaries on the progress of our attackers. We met in the Stromness Hotel for a drink during which a Midshipman accosted him, demanding to be allowed to be by himself on watch. The Captain told him to return on board but he kept on arguing. I went to the bar to get more beers and this idiot actually approached me to tell me that his daddy owned a castle; I really hope that this man decided not to stay at sea. The gunnery officer was Sub Lt Lustig Preen, I was most surprised to see him several years later on television championing the gay rights movement and challenging the government over the Services' treatment of gays. He never looked comfortable on the ship and was ruthlessly criticised by all and sundry. His name came from a prominent Austrian family and he had a string of names with links to the Hohenzollerns and Habsburgs. As he knew it was illegal to be homosexual in the Services at that time I believe that it was wrong of him to take the action that he has embarked upon. The First Lieutenant or Jimmy had been a manager of a whiskey distillery on Ilsay and was a larger-than-life character. With the personalities we had on the ship it was not surprising that we were going to encounter problems. Now that I am older I appreciate the difficulties of the Captain in his efforts to hold it all together. He must have found that leaving the ship to go on leave must have been a big worry for him.

As I had not had my full quota of shore time I was to spend only one year instead of eighteen months on the ship; that year seemed much longer. It is significant that when I was offered to return to the Orkney in 1987 I declined the offer and chose another ship; at the time I had a choice of 4 vessels so the Navy must have been getting short of people.

During the summer I acted as boarding party on several fishing boats. Whilst I enjoyed the job – measuring nets and learning to identify different fish – I began to question what we were doing. Due to MAFF rules, which originated in Brussels, I watched perfectly good fish being disposed of over the side as time after time fishermen exceeded their quotas. It soon became apparent that whilst British fishermen were being hounded by the Royal Navy at sea and the authorities ashore, other nationalities were not so regulated.

We boarded a Spanish fishing boat called the 'Montemaigmo' registered in Vigo; the Spanish skipper became very vocal and had to be calmed down, and the reason soon became clear. The boat was in a terrible mess, empty bottles of wine rolled around the mess space, the toilet was blocked and a large lump of mouldy cheese resided on the table which was very grimy; the reader must imagine the smell as I do not feel equal to describing it in print. The paperwork was non-existent, the nets too small, the fish boxes overflowing and ungutted (I was told this would end up as fertiliser) and the crew ran around the deck in bare feet. The ship was arrested and we headed towards Falmouth with the *Orkney* behind and the trawler's crew out of sight. At about 0300 one of the crew brought me a coffee; I was on the wheel taking course alterations from the Officer of the Watch on the *Orkney* as there was no autopilot. The man was clearly very ill with large scabs on his arms and legs. We anchored off Falmouth and the Customs Officers came on-board, he took one look at the crew man and said, 'Leprosy'. I have no idea what he was finally diagnosed as having, but an ambulance took him to hospital when we moored alongside. The court case took several days and in one pub, the Oddfellows Arms, we were royally treated. In the year I spent on the *Orkney* we arrested a total of two trawlers, both Spanish and cautioned a Dutch trawler for fishing too near a North Sea oil rig, I therefore doubt our effectiveness.

RN – END OF THE LINE, 1984–89

We were often diverted to other duties, which were also of questionable worth. On one occasion we chased a Russian submarine on the surface right up the coast of Norway. When he dived we lost him, as we were not fitted with sonar. One of our officers had noticed that she had a different ladder on her conning tower from the one in the book. On another embarrassing occasion we had to escort an elderly Ton-class minesweeper from Portsmouth to Rosyth as she was reduced to one engine, we had to signal a request to her to slow down. Halfway up the North Sea disaster struck, a lube oil pipe burst and showered the engine room with 1,000 litres of oil. Oil got in everywhere and we had to stop, releasing our anchor very close to a submarine cable. After opening and cleaning all kinds of electrical equipment in the engine room and repairing the pipe it was time to leave. The winch was started to pull the anchor up when the drive was suddenly catapulted in the air, landing with a crunch on the forecastle and only narrowly missing the Leading Seaman; the anchor was dropped with a marker buoy and we had to return with divers later to retrieve it.

The saddest duty was looking for fishermen who had gone over the side. The chances of finding anyone alive, particularly off the Shetlands, were slim but everyone volunteered in the hope of catching sight of a bobbing head or bright orange lifejacket. Prior to my joining the vessel several bodies had been recovered in the English Channel, but no one living. Ships would form into lines, areas of sea would be combed for hours; it was extremely disheartening to give up the search as we all approached the task with optimism.

Lord O'Hagan joined the ship; he was to be the new Fisheries Minister. After being seasick, he addressed the ship's company saying that he had just been appointed Fisheries Minister but had no idea of what it was all about. I remember thinking what a waste of time he was. Nothing constructive happened and when I took part in fishery protection duties three years later I was not surprised to find that we were dealing with the same problems.

In December 1984 we dry-docked in the synchrolift in Rosyth. The ship would be positioned on a cradle and lifted clear of the water then taken on rails into large sheds. This was by far the best dry-docking I have encountered with no problems painting the ship's hull caused by weather.

I was sent on an armed boarding course, which mainly consisted of watching films and stripping various weapons, mainly the Browning 9mm pistol and the awful 9mm sub-machine gun that was always considered more of a danger to those carrying it than any enemy. I instructed my mechanic that when he was behind me he was always to have his SMG unloaded.

The ship came out of dry-dock and was worked up by the Flag Officer Sea Training Staff or FOST. At the end of a less-than-perfect work-up we proceeded to Gibraltar for a NATO exercise. I once again took part in the top of the rock race, achieving it in just less than twenty-seven minutes. This was where the fun began. A large mooring buoy was adrift in the Bay of Biscay and it was decided that, as it was a navigational hazard, we were to sink it. General purpose machine guns were mounted on the bridge wing and soon bullets were bouncing off the structure. These were joined by 40mm Bofor shells, not very effective due to being designed for the anti-aircraft roll and being bounced around on a small ship. Attempts were made to sink it with plastic explosive, but to no avail the whole episode was farcical. The buoy was filled with a kind of polystyrene foam. Luckily the whole sorry affair was brought to an end when it was suggested that petrol be poured in from one of the Searider fuel tanks and then set on fire. I cannot remember whether this idea was ever suggested to the Captain; I certainly would not have been brave enough as the man was clearly getting more bad tempered with every passing day. I was ordered to take charge of the stokers washing the funnel. I could not understand why until I saw the Captain dripping wet from being hosed and the culprits doubled up with laughter.

In that year of 1985 I was more and more aware of the breakdown of naval discipline. A party on the Isle of Man resulted in the wardroom descending into scenes of Bacchanalia – a young lady with green spiky hair having been inadvertently invited onboard was doing unusual things with condoms. The next morning the stewards were cleaning exploded condoms from the deck head. A visit in Dover also ended in disaster and I could not wait to get ashore, one of the reasons being that my boss in harbour training ships, where I had been decidedly unhappy, had arrived on the *Orkney* and I began to wonder if it was me that was difficult.

Despite asking the Navy to remain in Rosyth on leaving the *Orkney* I was posted to a shore position in Portsmouth, which meant that my family had to be moved down south again. I appealed but apparently there were no shore jobs in Rosyth so off I went to Portsmouth. This proved to be a good move and the next eighteen months were the happiest I spent in the Navy. I was to be an Instructor in Damage Control at Phoenix NBCD School.

The Damage Repair Instructional Unit or DRIU was a large metal box positioned over a reservoir of water. Inside it resembled two decks split into four compartments into which water could be directed through various gaps arranged like splinter holes, fire main splits and sprung hatches to a supposed lower level that was flooded. We had portable pumps to restore fire main pressure and a number of different incidents on which we would teach the current thinking on how to deal with them. The structure itself was hinged on one side and hydraulic rams could tilt the unit resembling the actions of a sinking ship. One of the compartments could be set on fire and correct methods of entering and dealing with those fires was also taught.

A typical day would be three lectures by the instructors in the morning followed by an exercise. We would pitch the lectures and exercise according to the experience of the class, teenage juniors not being expected to have the same expertise as a class of Senior Ratings. We not only instructed British sailors but other nationals including the Nigerian, Indian, New Zealand and Malaysian navies to name but a few. At weekends we would on occasion play host to the Royal Navy Reserve. In the middle of one such exercise a bedraggled Lieutenant lurched through the smoke, noise and darkness to inform me that he was a chartered accountant; he was reminded that as he was now in the Navy we were not interested and to get on with what he was supposed to be doing.

We had a few dramas, to be expected in such a dramatic atmosphere. At the start of the exercise the class would be placed in the damage control station in the top level, a sledgehammer would be struck against the side of the DRIU, while at the same time I would throw two thunderflashes and broadcast the warning, 'air raid warning red, air raid warning red, brace, brace, brace!' Turn off all lighting, start the smoke machine and open the valve to the fire main split which would drench the class with water at 100 pounds per square inch. One team would search the lower compartment for leaks (which by now would be rapidly filling with water), another would deal with the fire main split by isolating and bridging it, and another would start the pumps and rig up temporary electrical supplies. During this initial five minutes the hydraulic pumps would be started and the DRIU would start to heel over to about 15 degrees from horizontal. To several visitors who could view from a gallery, which only got a little wet, including the BBC it appeared chaotic, but as long as people were taught how to use equipment most courses achieved the objective. In more advanced courses if anyone looked too good, we would remove them to test the chain of command; we always nominated a leader.

There were problems with some courses, especially RFA crews who would occasionally rebel at being told what to do. Having had to work on an abandoned RFA in the Falklands which only narrowly avoided being sunk because of the swift action of those on board, I never understood why lessons learnt could be objected to. We also had a problem with the Nigerian officers who would complain that the water was too cold and retire without taking part. One Malaysian team panicked on seeing the fire and jumped out of the loading door onto the concrete below, breaking some limbs on the way. One British team of young officers in training had a narrow escape when one of them dropped his hose that was on water wall shielding his partner from the fire. On this occasion the only damage was some singed eyebrows and frayed tempers. Most classes responded positively, on some occasions suggesting different ways of doing things which we always encouraged and welcomed, evaluating each idea before inclusion in the course.

There were three permanent instructors there: Al Davies the Chief Stoker and senior instructor, Daisy May, a Petty Officer, and myself. We all got on very well for the eighteen months I was at Phoenix and it has always been my opinion that, had I been allowed to stay at Phoenix, I would not have left the Navy. A new DRIU was being built in Southampton to be delivered to HMS *Raleigh* and was so big it had to be taken in sections. We helped with the design, as many incidents were just not realistic. I with the Electrical System, and Al, who laughed when he saw perfectly round splinter holes with no ragged edges, gave our expertise. It had been made that way because it was feared that people might cut themselves on sharp edges. We pointed out that we did not have this problem in our own DRIU that had been realistically designed. For the first time since the *Fearless* I felt that I was doing something worthwhile that may in the future help someone to react correctly in a difficult situation. Ships do not only get damaged by enemy action; fire is a real problem at sea and with the number of ships increasing as well as the number of poorly trained or in some instances untrained crews, collision and grounding is on the increase.

Taking part in a first aid course I was put on shifts with the Accident and Emergency department of a Portsmouth civilian hospital. I was amazed and humbled by what the nurses had to put up with. Drug overdoses, timewasters, angry and abusive patients and still they were able to show sympathy to a DIY 'expert' who had to have his hand stitched up. I would not do the job and wonder at the sanity of those who do.

The final months in Phoenix were hectic; I was given the choice of four ships including HMS *Leeds Castle*, an Island-class offshore patrol vessel which I chose. As one of my duties was to be Captain of the Flight Deck I was put on a small aircraft course in Portland. My final act was to inspect the new DRIU in Raleigh with Daisy May. We had trained the instructors and I was impressed to see how they had adapted to the new unit which was very much superior to our own. It was bigger for a start off and could be tilted port or starboard to an angle of 20 degrees from horizontal.

At the same time I was moving my family back to Rosyth (no seagoing drafts having been available in Portsmouth). Complications arose when my wife's car was rammed by a truck on the way north. I missed my flight to Rotterdam, and the Navy arranged for me to join in the North Sea by helicopter. I duly made my way to Norwich Airport and waited in the passengers' lounge. There was a loud noise and a helicopter landed, the aircrewman came in and supplied me with flying overalls and a helmet and much to the astonishment of onlookers I threw my bags in and we took off.

I had joined *Phoenix* on the 4 September 1985 and left on 26 May 1987. I had done well and was in good spirits. I joined a karate club, and took part in distance running. Life was good and with ten years left in the Navy I was extremely happy, but four months later I submitted my request to be discharged from the navy with eighteen months' notice.

I relieved Chris Beard who I had first met as a mechanic on HMS *Bristol*; he did not relish his duties on the flight deck, and had lost all faith in the Royal Navy. It is significant that Chris had submitted his eighteen-month notice for discharge from the RN, as did many others including myself.

For missing my flight I was fined £40. The stupidity of being charged was proven when the Captain told me that, having reviewed my movements and duties at the time, it was extremely unlikely that I would have been able to meet with the schedule, but he would have to fine me. The use of the helicopter was also pointless as two days later we were to arrive in Portland, where I could have joined the ship with ease. I was becoming annoyed and the doubts I had on the *Orkney* re-surfaced. I spent 20 months on the *Leeds Castle*, which were to convince me that the Navy was finished, and descending into beaurocratic chaos.

I soon learned that HMS *Dumbarton Castle*, affectionately known as the Dumbo and sister ship of the *Leeds* was in the Falklands and that we were going to have to replace her, which we subsequently did. After some fishery protection duties we headed for Rosyth and the synchrolift for a dry-dock.

The *Leeds Castle* was built in 1981 in Hall Russell of Aberdeen. She was armed with one 40mm Bofors but had a large flight deck and could be used to lay mines. She had two Ruston Paxman main engines but unlike the *Orkney* had two shafts; once again I was surprised to find that she could only just make 19 knots which seems slow for a patrol ship. Since leaving the Navy I have served on many merchant ships that could outrun her. The weapons fit was OK for fishery protection but I admit to having been a little perplexed at having to go to the Falklands in such an unprotected vessel, that had been built by a shipyard more accustomed to fishing vessels, tugs and oil rig supply boats. During the dry-dock the gun was changed for a 30mm Oto Melara that while being superior to the Bofors was hardly likely to ward off an air attack. Had I known what one of our duties was to be it is doubtful whether I would have sailed at all – honour in combat is all very well if you have a fighting chance.

Spares were always difficult to come by, we would order new light fittings from naval stores who would give us an estimate of three years to fulfil. I later probed Thorn EMI and in the end naval stores had to admit that the order had been cancelled. Time after time these difficulties arose with a civilian in PSTON deciding without consultation or even stepping on the ship to supply or not. I became more and more frustrated; the Chief Engineer would give no support but would only complain that things did not work. We eventually started talking and he agreed that certain items were past repair. Despite his and the Captain's support naval stores would not be changed. As I spoke to other ships in Rosyth it soon became clear that ours was not the only ship facing shortages and outrageous beaurocracy. Our main priority was to make sure that we would be able to operate safely and effectively in the inhospitable South Atlantic with a minimum of support. The ship was to stay in those waters for eighteen months and what we did now would severely affect the success or failure of the tasks allotted to her.

Another problem was that now the dockyard was a commercial enterprise of Babcock Thorn, every task was costed commercially. This was the first time that I ever saw a warship treated in such a way. Warships should not be treated like merchant ships with respect to repair and maintenance, and when they are more money is spent putting things right later. This was proven when a repair on a generator, which I had requested, was deemed not necessary; this later failed and the ship was denied the use of a generator.

To highlight the problems faced, an incident at the end of the docking period demonstrates the absurdity of the situation we found ourselves in. A load barge had been hired to come alongside, which cost money. During the subsequent trial I discovered that a circuit board was defective, we had no spare so I looked in the books and found that the only other ship which used this board was 8,000 miles away. I also found that there was a spare in Rosyth. As this board could be changed in ten minutes I visited the stores office in Rosyth. I was told that as this was Friday I could have the new one on Monday. This would have entailed calling back the barge to set it up; the stores people told me that a new one could be sent from another depot. I enquired as to why I could not have it now, they replied that they were holding it as an emergency spare. I pointed out that we were the only ship that could use it in the northern hemisphere, but they remained unmoved and no amount of rational argument could change the decision. And so the taxpayer paid for the barge to return the following Monday but we had to wait for a WREN driver to bring it so we wasted even more time. My decision to escape from this madhouse was looking ever more sensible even though I had no idea what I would do in civilian life.

A bout of salmonella kept me off work for three months. Misdiagnosis by the sick bay at HMS *Cochrane* (the barracks ashore) meant that I was transferred to a real hospital later than I should have been. I lost 3 stone and was very ill. Luckily for the ship the man who was to relieve me was currently in the Rosyth Fleet Maintenance Group so he got a good look round the ship. Even after I returned to work I was ill for some time afterwards lasting from December 1987 to April 1988.

It was time to get fit. Susan Jennings, a friend of my wife who she had gone to school with had developed cancer. I had known Sue since I was fourteen and resolved to get off my back and do something. My wife and I trained for the Dunfermline Half Marathon due in June 1988. We trained and completed many 5-mile and 8-mile runs and felt confident on the day. After 12.5 miles my wife collapsed. I supported her as she struggled for the finishing line at 13.5 miles. An X-ray showed that she had a stress fracture of her leg, which was a serious problem. My First Lieutenant said that I could not be spared despite the fact that we were not to go to sea for another seven weeks and my relief was actually in the dockyard. Naval welfare assessed that my wife was unable to look after the children with a leg in plaster and they would have to be taken into care. I exploded and was granted leave to look after her. She was a Beavers leader and had been instrumental in organising an annual children's parade through Dunfermline ending with a picnic in Pittencrieff Park. A wheelchair was produced along with transport and I wheeled her through Dunfermline. Her story was printed in the *Dunfermline Press* and the *Glasgow Herald*, we raised a few hundred pounds for cancer research and once again I felt powerless to do anything else. Susan is 'in remission' from her cancer which after a lot of treatment has not returned.

After a rededication ceremony we started working up, drills and exercises began in Rosyth and ended in Portland. The ship stopped in London and we tied up alongside HMS *Belfast* where we played host to a group of people called the Fisherman's Guild, as to be expected in London there was not one seaman among them. They caused a lot of work when one idiot dropped a glass of sherry into the Autopilot. I suspect that like the visit by Lord O'Hagan on the *Orkney*, this achieved nothing. European quotas and rules are still playing havoc with our fishing industry, the Spanish still openly flout those rules and the UK Government, as usual, are penalising the very people who elected them to serve.

At about this time I was asked to take over the running of the ship's tobacco from another Petty Officer; I had no idea why. This particular man had been a friend of mine, we would go ashore together and generally got on well. As I inspected the books in readiness to take over I gradually realised with growing horror that there was a lot missing. On the *Orkney* a Customs officer had made me go through the books to find 200 cigarettes, which I found to be a minor mistake carried over from three months earlier before I had taken over. On *Leeds Castle* it was no minor mistake, there were thousands of cigarettes missing. My friend pleaded with me to cover it up but I knew from the numbers involved and the checks made that this would be impossible. I approached the First Lieutenant and we went through the books time and again. The Petty Officer had fooled the young Sub-Lieutenant who was supposed to be the supervisor and we soon had the Special Investigation Branch on board. His defence at the inquiry was that he was 'bad at maths'.

We headed south and were just turning into Biscay when a helicopter crashed into the sea, having taken off from the RFA Fort Grange. We spent all night searching for survivors and retrieving wreckage. Our only port of call on the way to the Falklands was Gibraltar where we met HMS *Amazon* a Type-21 frigate. The only other stop after that was at Ascension Island to take on fuel from a tanker called the *Maersk Ascension*. I sympathised with the officers and crew who visited us – four months stuck in one place must have been incredibly boring. We had considerable trouble removing the Chief Engineer from our bar; he had become very attached to it. As we headed south she roared past flashing cheeky signals about how she would be in Port Stanley first. The next time I saw her she was limping back to Gibraltar, while we arrived first, a real tortoise and hare story.

In December we found ourselves off the coast of Argentina patrolling up and down, the last time I ever took part in action stations. Back in the Falklands things had improved greatly for the troops, they had been moved out of Port Stanley and into purpose-built comfortable accommodation. The airport could take all kinds of aircraft having been extended, the NAAFI had a shopping complex and bars, and the road to it was no longer made of mud. We loaded up with stores for an interesting expedition to South Georgia having embarked two Japanese scientists and Bob Headland, a scientist working for the British Antarctic Survey. Bob was excellent; I particularly remember a lecture he gave on Shackleton's expedition of 1912, and another he gave on the flora and fauna of South Georgia. Bob informed me that there are forty different types of grass on South Georgia – if only my schoolteachers had been as enthusiastic about their subjects as Bob was about his. He was also partial to a glass of Scotch; I never tired of listening to him.

Another interesting passenger was the grandson of the man who had built the church in Grytviken in 1913. The Royal Engineers had repaired the church and they had done a really good job. On Christmas Eve 1988 we made our way along the beach past all the whalebones and sat in the church for the service, some of which was conducted in Norwegian. Pictures were relayed via the ship to Norway; I found it all extremely moving.

The ship left Grytviken and sailed around to Leith, another abandoned whaling station, and I had to return on board for a repair to the controllable pitch propeller. Sailing back to the Falklands we met up with HMS *Endurance* who had a narrow escape after collision with an Iceberg.

Back in the Falklands I had the most incredible luck by being seconded to work on a ship called the *Stena Seaspread*. My time in the Navy was rapidly coming to a close and I cursed the luck that had sent me to the Falklands where I had little prospect of finding alternative employment. After working with the Electrical Officer on the ship I was invited to partake in a glass of whiskey. This turned out to be one of the most profitable rounds of drinks I have ever had, and I didn't even have to pay for it. The Electrical Officer gave me a list of about 50 addresses of merchant shipping companies. I had already constructed a curriculum vitae, which my wife had typed up. With addresses gained from looking at labels on Electrical Equipment and those from the *Stena Seaspread*, added to another few I had obtained from a fishery protection officer, I had over 200 contact addresses. My shipmates told me that I would be unsuccessful, but I sent them to my wife who typed letters to all 200.

The *Stena Seaspread* was being used as a mobile repair base although she was capable of much more, being fitted with a flight deck above the bridge and a diving bell. There was a Royal Navy team living on the ship. I saw the electricians doing very odd things with batteries so I enquired as to who ordered them to dunk batteries in the sea. 'OSLO', they replied. When I asked who OSLO was they told me it stood for the Outer Space Liaison Officer. He was certainly very strange and I declined an offer of his help on our ship preferring to do the work myself.

Just before my relief arrived I was presented with a piece of paper offering me an extension to my original twenty-two years of service so that I could stay in the Navy until the age of fifty. I saw the Captain, told him of my decision to go and no more was said. My relief, who had been on the ship in Rosyth during my illness, arrived. I had known Mickey for some time as we had been on Fleet Maintenance Group in Portsmouth together in 1979. We still had to hand over. In addition to my job as senior electrician I was also the Captain of the Flight Deck, Film Officer, and I ran the ship's tobacco store all of which involved a lot of paperwork.

Eventually all was complete, I left the ship and embarked on an RAF transport, stopping only briefly at Ascension then on to Brize Norton. At Brize I managed to find transport to Heathrow where I boarded a flight to Edinburgh. I had some leave due that would take me from 6 January 1989 to 13 March 1989. The only thing left to do was take my kit to HMS *Cochrane* and spend a day leaving the Navy. I joined a class of all different rates including WRNS. I remember being the only one who had the firm offer of a job. One Chief Petty Officer was complaining that he had sent five CV off without a job offer; when I told him of my 200 he was taken aback.

When I arrived home letters were already starting to land on my doormat. Mostly they were advising me to find employment elsewhere, but 20% were asking me to interview. Before attending Cochrane my first foray into the world of civilian employment was in Hull having been called in to see Marrs, an old trawler company who had diversified into survey and fishery protection duties. I was told I could join the *Criscilla*, which like the Orkney had been constructed by Hall Russell of Aberdeen. I never heard another word so I suspect that I was less than impressive. Another company called C.I. Shipping had written to me advising me that due to the reduction in the number of ships there were no positions, but a week later I was asked to attend the office in London for an interview immediately. As I left the underground station nearest the office I bumped into Tony Sheehan who I had last seen on the *Fearless*. He was working for London Underground on the elevators as they had fallen into disrepair, tragically ending in the fire at King's Cross station.

I made my way to the office and was given a cup of tea. Two Superintendents interviewed me and I was informed that I had to fly out to Dubai as soon as possible. One of them had spotted my CV screwed up in the bin of the Personnel Officer, spotted the words cranes and winches, the Personnel Officer was rebuked and I was hurriedly employed. The pay was tax free and in US$, the contract duration was six months followed by three months unpaid leave and I was to have the rank of Electrical Officer. I could not believe my luck, as I was joining the Merchant Navy, albeit Bermudan flag. I knew I would not be liable to reserve service. The effort put in to find one Petty Officer Electrician would not be worth it. There were a few hurdles to overcome, despite having been passed fit for military service I still had to have an ENG 1 medical; I also needed a seaman's discharge book and a seaman's identity card. A uniform list was provided and I went out and bought a lot of uniform that was really not needed

After the interview I was offered a hotel for the night but I elected to head straight for home, there were an awful lot of things to do. On arriving at home my wife told me to telephone another company that night with regard to a job in a power station in Saudi Arabia but I declined the offer having already accepted the job with C.I. Shipping.

The following Tuesday I walked out of barracks with not a glance back, I knew that for a couple of years I could always return as many did. One of my friends had left to work for Camper and Nicholson's building yachts, but six months later he was back in the Navy. I knew it was going to be hard going but I was determined to succeed. In one day I arranged a date for leaving my married quarter, found an accountant and arranged a mortgage and my affairs so that my wife could buy a house. A few days later, having satisfied all paperwork and having been given the relevant inoculations, I left Edinburgh Airport on my way to Dubai on 17 February 1989.

Officially I was still on leave from the Navy for another month but I was allowed to go, there being no point in me attending any more so called naval resettlement courses. I had asked how long the handover would be, and was told that unlike the Royal Navy who insisted on at least a three-day handover, I would be expected to take over the duties of Electrical Officer on the same day. As it turned out this was not difficult but I must admit to being a little concerned. After 13 years and 6 months in the Navy I had known nothing else but on no occasion did I consider going back.

My father by this time was working for the Director General Ships Refitting and was moving to Rosyth himself. He retired from Rosyth as a Director Grade 7 in the Ministry of Defence having moved around the country in various positions. The only member of the family still at sea was myself as Uncle Robert had also left the Navy.

CHAPTER VII

CI Shipping, February 1989 to June 1990

I WAS MET AT DUBAI AIRPORT by an agent's runner and after a few formalities was taken to the port of Sharjah to join the MV *Meltem*, an aging Refrigerated Cargo Ship known as a Reefer. The *Meltem* seemed to me to be a very odd name for a ship designed to keep things frozen; it was actually named after the Meltemi wind that blows through Turkey. She was painted white and looked huge to me despite only having a gross registered tonnage of 6,883 tonnes. Built in Rotterdam in 1968 as the SA *Zebedeilah* she was certainly showing her age. I could see that there were only winches and derricks instead of cranes discharging cargo from her six hatches.

The run was regular, starting in Paranagua, Brazil with a cargo of frozen chickens and then calling at Durban for oranges, then Kismayu in Somalia to load bananas and watermelons, with a discharge in the Gulf of Iran starting at Sharjah then Bahrain, Damman and Kuwait.

I was shown to my cabin and apologised to for the lack of space. Far from being disappointed I was happy to see that I had my own shower and toilet, a bed and a day bed. I had not lived in this much luxury on a ship since the trip on the *Uganda* in 1983. All the ship's electrical drawings were under my bunk in various states of decay, along with some broken electrical bits which I removed. The chap I was relieving lived in Brazil with his Brazilian wife; looking at his notes I soon discovered he had some extremely strange ideas.

The first thing I noticed was a hostility to the RN. It took me sometime to get used to this but in the end I think the experience of sailing on this ship provided me with a lot of fortitude when confronted with other merchant vessels in a similar state of decay. The winches broke down regularly and it was only after a lot of hard work that I managed to keep them working in one port without a breakdown. She was not as complicated as a naval vessel but there was never a shortage of things to do. The first hurdle was the other officers – if I walked past a piece of equipment that later broke down I was blamed for it. It was not long before I became as thick skinned as the rest of them and started telling people where to get off. This method of abuse must be effective, as I have no friends from the Royal Navy where friendships are transient but still keep in contact with Gavin Swadel, then Second Officer and now Captain of the motor tug *Cramond* on the Firth of Forth. They really were the most odd bunch of people but I admit to still feeling a little nostalgic about that trip despite the problems we had.

The crew came from Bangladesh and seemed in a perpetual state of confusion. We had two Bangladeshi officers who rarely spoke to each other, one being Moslem the other Hindi, and two Philippino engineers. There were eight British officers including myself and I have no idea as to how many crew were on board. Their contracts lasted for a year and on occasion they would stay on the ship for longer periods.

At two o'clock one morning shortly after joining I was awakened by the on-watch greaser who stood at my door complete with lifejacket saying, 'Number two generator, maybe sometime big fire'. I called the Chief Engineer and we went to help the Third Engineer who was on watch. Some leaking fuel had been dripping onto a hot exhaust pipe lagging, and the fire was soon extinguished. When I asked where the crew were I was greeted with howls of derision. They were all sitting in the lifeboat with their bags packed; I have no idea who they thought was going to launch the boat for them. I was shocked, having been used to everyone being very conscientious about fire drills and taking the right action – this was new territory for me. After asking the Chief Officer if I could give some lectures and run some exercises I was encouraged by the enthusiasm shown by the crew, but my hopes were dashed when on every occasion they would head for the lifeboats. I soon realised that I was wasting my time and had to agree with the Chief Engineer who had been amused by my naivety that it was a lost cause. Another problem was that they would not wear any safety gear. I was told by the Deck Sarang that Allah would decide if they would have an accident or not, therefore there was no point in wearing goggles, safety boots or helmet. My answer was that Allah had also provided this equipment for them to use, but the idea never caught on. No amount of argument could convince them that they were wrong.

We regularly called into Kismayu, where the crew would be warned to lock all doors and not to trade with the Somalis as they used to steal everything, which is not a comment on race but a fact. The crew would ignore the warning and then after leaving the port would bemoan the fact that they had had everything stolen.

Some of the officers were not much better, an argument I witnessed over the ownership of some crayfish between the Second Engineer and the Chief Officer was a classic. A Somali had sold some crayfish to the Mate for some old rope, the Mate left the Somali who then sold the same bucket of crayfish to the Second Engineer for some old oil drums. The argument that followed was very entertaining, providing us with hours of amusement.

Most of our problems would start in the Gulf for several reasons. We were not allowed alcohol, not allowed ashore and in Kuwait would often have our cabins searched in the middle of the night for contraband alcohol or pornography; this covered even newspapers like the *Sun*, and several papers would be confiscated. We all hated Kuwait and Dammam where we were treated worse than criminals. Even the simple act of taking the draught marks, which the Mate had to do during discharge and prior to sailing was, on occasion, stopped by the armed guard on the gangway. This would only be allowed if soft drinks, and a chair, were sent down to the guard. In Kuwait a Bangladeshi Fourth Engineer threw a can of coke into the harbour. I managed to stop the Kuwaiti from taking him to jail, but we had to pay several cartons of cigarettes to keep him. The harbour was in a terrible state with dead sheep from the Australian sheep carriers floating in the heavily polluted water. Pakistani stevedores would work all day in the heat watched by a Kuwaiti in an air-conditioned car. Towards the end of their shift they would tire in the terrible heat; if they flagged the Kuwaiti would jump out of his car and beat them around the head. When Saddam Hussein invaded Kuwait I was glad that I was no longer in the armed forces as to fight for these people would have left a bad taste in my mouth. When another mosque is erected in this country it should be remembered that a Christian Church could not be erected in Saudi Arabia.

Bahrain was a different matter, the only problem being with the Saudi Arabians crowded around bars getting silly on two beers. We used to visit the British Club in Bahrain, which had a swimming pool and gardens. At the other end of the run was Paranagua in the state of Parana, a scruffy place where the rain would pour sometimes for days, preventing us from loading cargo. One night I was heading back to the ship, so much rain had fallen that the taxi refused to go to the port through the large puddles. I rolled up my trousers, took off my shoes and socks and waded through. In the light given off by the port floodlights I could see fish swimming around. I associated Paranagua with piranha and ran for my life though I later found out that there were no piranhas there (different spelling).

A Greek repair Engineer approached me asking how many defective motors I had on board: none was the wrong answer. It transpired that good motors had been landed ashore, left on a bench and returned to the ship having had nothing done to them. The cost of repair borne by the company would then go into people's pockets. I declined the offer. Whilst visiting Paranagua on another ship several years later I learned

MV Scirocco Universal in Egion, Greece, 14 March 1990

that he had been shot dead; the repair engineers who then attended us were Italians who had taken over the business.

In Paranagua we were informed that a character called the Moon Man was to join the ship to replace the Third Engineer. I was curious as to why he was called the Moon Man, 'you will find out' they all said. I certainly did an extremely tall thin man unfolded himself from the taxi and lurched towards the ship. He was the strangest human being I have ever met, his head would slowly gyrate and he walked with a curious motion as if lighter than air, hence the Moon Man. No one could understand what I took to be a Scottish accent including the Scots we had on board. The Captain would wave his hand in front of the Moon Man's face and inquire as to whether he was in today or not. We played Trivial Pursuit which he usually won as he insisted on reading the questions which nobody could understand. Another character was Pottsy, then Third Engineer Reefer. The Captain insisted on his officers being in uniform at evening meal. Pottsy, a Geordie living in Brazil, would join the ship dressed in t-shirt and shorts wearing flip flops and carrying a small carrier bag. The Captain would say, 'I hope you have your uniform, Mr Potts.' Pottsy would reply in the affirmative saying that he would be present at dinner, but he never was. With a cargo of chickens kept at −25 degrees centigrade and Oranges kept at +6 it had been known for Reefer Engineers to get mixed up. Pottsy would take a chicken and defrost it in the microwave and freeze an orange in the freezer overnight then with a worried look present them to the Chief Engineer who would fly into a panic. Another of Pottsy's habits was to set fire to his cabin as he persisted in smoking in bed. His wife was Brazilian and extremely volatile. As they were in the cabin next door to me I could hear heavy objects being thrown around the cabin accompanied by howls of pain or derision; I could not tell the difference and tried hard to ignore it. Whilst he was looking after the cargo I never heard of any problems and believe he was allowed to get away with a lot because of his competence.

The chickens we carried from Brazil were reported to be full of hormones and it was widely rumoured that one of the ship's Pursers had fed cargo chicken to the officers and crew with the result that they had all grown breasts. Stevedores would urinate on the cargo and I have always washed fruit since.

As the months went on we were told that we were to go to dry dock in Durban, South Africa where I was asked to stay on the ship for a few weeks more than my six months to help with the large amount of work required to be done. In Durban my relief joined. I discovered that I was the youngest Electrical Officer in the company and the best behaved. The first night on the ship he managed to get himself and the Electrical Officer of the sister ship *Mistral* arrested by the South African Police whilst brawling in the streets.

Our Chief Engineer had changed from the one who was on board when I joined and was known as Fingers after his habit of interfering with settings and adjusting things for no apparent reason, usually causing lots of work for everyone else. The Second Mate had also changed to Bill Laverick who I immediately got on with. The last I heard of Bill he was a Captain of a reefer. Contractors inadvertently set off the CO_2 fire fighting system so Bill and I put on breathing apparatus to check that no one had been caught below decks and was in trouble; no one knew how many people were on board. Naked Africans were cleaning bilges and tanks in large numbers and nobody seemed to care who was there. Fingers had been helping us with our breathing apparatus but when I entered the CO_2 room to try and turn off the valve he walked off. If I had been in trouble there would have been no one to help me. As this had been the actions of a Chief Engineer I was extremely cautious about who I trusted in hazardous conditions.

I enjoyed Durban, we did get some time off to go shopping and I soon developed a taste for Kingclip, which is a very tasty fish. I especially enjoyed a dish called Kingclip Fantastic, which consisted of Kingclip in a prawn-based sauce. This was the place where I first discovered that I liked wine, and I have enjoyed Cabernet Sauvignon ever since along with a lot of other wines I had been ignorant of.

The state of the *Meltem* had been a revelation, the fire main had been repaired so many times with temporary cement boxes that there was very little pipe left. On 22 August 1989 I left the ship in Durban and went home for two and a half months leave. I knew that to get employment in another company it would be better if I were offered another contract with CI so after two months I awaited the telephone call as I was now short of money.

In November 1989 I was instructed to join the MV *Scirrocco Universal*, another reefer and again in Sharjah. This ship was far removed from what I now thought to be the company norm. Built in 1979 in Japan she was, as far as I am concerned, the best ship I have ever sailed on.

Mistakes made by the company in later years (mainly with selection of personnel) reduced her to an unreliable mess when I next saw her in 1997, but in 1989 things were different. She had a respectable speed of 22 knots powered by a Mitsubishi Sulzer slow-speed engine. Control was electronic/pneumatic, which we did on occasion have problems with. The automatic STAL refrigeration plant was not fully working but the Reefer Engineer and myself put everything right in the first month. Most of the hatches were served by winches due to the company's insistence with two cranes between #2 and #3 hatch, which could be Geminied, or joined together and controlled from one cab to lift heavier loads.

There was very little wrong and after the initial problems of temperature control of the refrigeration plant and the realisation that the engine control problem was due to water in the pneumatic system I was left with planned maintenance as my main priority. On the *Meltem* maintenance had been impossible, as my work had consisted of jumping from one defect to another. Unlike the *Meltem* the *Scirrocco* had what is called an unmanned machinery space otherwise known as a UMS ship. An alarm plant monitors all machinery with pressure, temperature, and level transducers and switches. Any alarm is transmitted to the duty engineer's cabin with secondary panels in the Officers' Mess and the bridge. If the alarm is not answered in the engine room within three minutes the alarm in the Chief Engineer's cabin sounds automatically. In the RN all machinery control rooms are manned and this was a first for me. My initial reservations were soon overcome due to the reliability of this system, which is regularly tested. Some ships I have served on since have had less than satisfactory systems. The willingness of some engineers to try and fool Lloyds surveyors into accepting that a defective system is in fact working correctly is amazing and dangerous. Some ships lose the right to use this system and watch-keeping officers have to be provided so that the engine room is manned twenty-four hours a day. On one ship I visited in 1998 I found that of a total of 120 alarms only ten were connected. British Engineers on the ship had concealed this fact from the company who after receiving my report changed the system.

To my pleasant surprise I found that Gavin was Second Mate, in general the ship was far happier and the people generally more competent. Living conditions were excellent, and my cabin was larger than I had ever had; there was also a swimming pool and the Officers Mess was extremely pleasant. Alistair McMaster took over as Captain (his first

Gavin Swadel, 2nd mate, and I, Scirocco Universal, 1989

command) shortly after I joined with a noisy Steve Harris as Chief Officer. It was to be some time before I managed to sail with such agreeable people again.

The schedule was hectic, we called at Mogadishu in Somalia, Jeddah in Saudi Arabia and then transited the Suez Canal (a first for me) calling at Patras and Naples before heading off for Paranagua. We spent Christmas Day at sea; I remember that the company provided Christmas crackers, which must have been a job lot as they all contained green party hats.

In Paranagua we anchored, and the Captain refused to pay the bribes expected of all ships entering South American ports. We stayed at anchor and eventually he had to bow to corruption. Spirits and tobacco poured off the ship in large quantities in the bags of pilots, agents and any number of port officials. We stayed in port over New Year playing football with the local nightclub bouncers who, with bare feet, easily evaded our working boots and royally trounced us 10-1, our only goal being scored by one of our Bangladeshi greasers.

During our visit the Captain had the unenviable task of informing me that my father-in-law had died. He was only sixty and had always

Christmas Dinner on Scirocco Universal (all the hats were green). From Right: Myself (Electrical Officer); Bangladeshi Steward; Steve Harris (Chief Officer); Gavin Swadel (Second Officer); Rick Hutchinson (Third Engineer).

been in the best of health, which had covered a weak heart. The agency let me telephone home from their offices; it was only after he had died that I fully appreciated him. We had not always got on but lately had become closer, and the realisation that the years wasted in argument could have been put to better use haunted me for some time, especially when alone in a ship's cabin.

We left Brazil and headed for the Straits of Magellan, which separate Tierra del Fuego from the southern tip of South America. Two years previously the ship had hit a rock ripping holes in the hatches. Divers in Punta Arenas had inspected the damage with a video camera; the copy of the video was shown with divers swimming into thousands of apples, which had been picked up in Valparaiso Chile. The trip through the Straits is impressive, narrow channels marked by the odd shipwreck as if a reminder that even with the advantages of modern navigational aids mistakes still occurred. The Chilean pilots were extremely professional and I listened with interest as in perfect English they told of the history

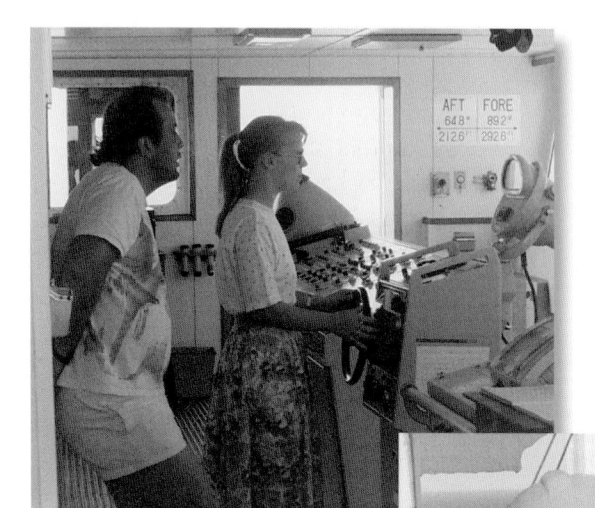

Gwen Steering with Bill Laverick, Second Officer Scirocco Universal

Gwen, Up a Crane, Scirocco Universal, 1990

Gwen kitted-up with safety belt on the MV Scirocco Universal 1990

of the Straits and the flora and fauna of an area they clearly loved. Several years later when transiting the Straits on another ship one of the pilots told me that a Royal Navy frigate (a Type-22) had refused a pilot and had ended up aground. During my association with the Merchant Navy I have often been embarrassed by the arrogance and incompetence of the RN, which sadly seems on the increase.

We docked in Valparaiso, another first. I was aware that I had spent virtually my whole naval career in either north Norway or the Falklands and had little experience of the more interesting parts of the world. For the aspiring traveller I would not recommend service in the Royal Navy and even merchant ships spend little time in port these days. The next generation of the country's mariners will be a dull lot indeed, with little knowledge of the ports they visit due to a combination of reduced manning meaning longer working hours and limited time in port with little chance of recreation. My contract was for six months which due to having eight British officers on the ship and stays in port of several days, was easily managed. Later in my career a four-month contract where I was the only Brit (the other officers being German and the crew Philippino) would drag on and on with little recreation as the companies, whilst boasting that they had made record profits, would continually seek to make savings on crew costs.

In Valparaiso we met a long-time friend of seamen in the form of Wolfgang Scheuber who owns the Hamburg Restaurant in Calle O'Higgins. He was an ex-cook in the Hamburg Amerika Line and his restaurant is a museum of all kinds of artefacts including old divers' helmets, photographs of Von Spee's squadron shortly before it won the battle of Coronel against the British and was subsequently annihilated at the Battle of the Falklands in 1914 on 8 December (which also happens to be my birthday). Wolfgang always treats visiting sailors well, and always gets the beers in. We presented him with the commissioning bottle from the *Scirrocco Universal*, which is still hanging up in the Hamburg. On his bar is an RNLI lifeboat; every year he collects the money and sends a cheque to them. He respects them for helping Seamen and is wildly enthusiastic for all things nautical. I last saw him in 1994 but he was still in business in the year 2000 as one of my son's friends visited the Hamburg. The sight of this short, stocky, bristle-headed man heading towards the ship always entertains me and I never tire of him holding his beer glass aloft and saying, 'Das ist der Seeman's leben, ja'. I have a

Gwen and Third Engineer's wife at Pompei, Mount Veruvius in background, 1990

lot of respect for Wolfgang and have always been royally entertained by him; he very often refuses payment for beer and food.

We left Valparaiso in a storm, one of the cranes could not be stowed properly and I had not been informed as I had been in the engine room. As the ship started to roll the Captain telephoned from the bridge to say that he was going to return to port unless the crane was stowed properly. The Chief Engineer and myself made our way across the deck and climbed the ladder to the crane. We managed with some difficulty to park the crane with me holding in contactors with a screwdriver with a lot of sparks whilst in the cab above the Chief gave instructions. We only narrowly avoided returning to port which saved the company a not insignificant amount of money. The machinery space was underneath the crane driver's seat and very often they would urinate and on occasion defecate into the machinery compartment. This time the crane driver had shorted out some low-voltage control circuits that I repaired before

Panama Canal, 1990

the next port. The smell was awful and several relays and contacts had to be replaced before the crane was operational. Due to the ports we visited our only method of loading and discharging cargo was by the ship's equipment and very often I was not allowed ashore. My solution was to carry a radio or telephone the agent to let him know my whereabouts as the engineers claimed to know nothing about cranes and winches.

Heading back through Magellan our next port of call was a brief stop in Durban. On the way past an island some South Africans had invited us to a barbecue – in Afrikaans 'brie', but the Captain refused.

My thoughts turned to home and I invited my wife to join me on the ship, her mother volunteering to look after our growing sons. She joined the ship in Sharjah and spent three months aboard. Not being one to sit in the sun she soon found a boiler suit and started working with me much to the bemusement of the crew who could not understand what Memsahib was doing. To her credit she repaired one crane controller, which gave no more problems for our remaining three months and updated a drawing of the fire alarm system, which was then mounted in the control room.

After visiting Mogadishu where we were invited onto a Kuwaiti tanker by its Bulgarian Captain. We loaded bananas in Kismayu then back to Jeddah and Suez. Gwen spent her birthday in Egion after which we spent a nice few days in Salerno. With the Third Engineer and his Sri Lankan wife we visited Pompeii, which was a real highlight. This time of course I had to make my own way by train unlike my earlier visit organised entirely by the Italian Navy.

After Salerno we picked up large rolls of paper in Las Palmas and then on to Panama; my wife's first trip through the Panama Canal was also mine. Diesel locomotives known as Mules positioned either side of the ship keep it central in the channel and two pilots stay on the bridge, the Panama Canal being one of the few places in the world where the pilots take full responsibility for the ship. It is very spectacular; as the water enters the locks you can feel the ship of several thousand tonnes rising beneath you, which feels very odd the first time it is experienced.

We headed down past Peru where we were approached by a Peruvian gunboat, then eventually anchored off Valparaiso. The mist came down and as it evaporated ships appeared out of the murk, at first just the tops then the vessels gradually emerged.

Valparaiso was an eye opener for Gwen, she had never seen ship's officers build a tower of chairs in a bar and write the ship's name on the ceiling. She also met Wolfgang and signed his visitor's book. Four years later her record was still there, I checked.

We spent a day in the resort of Vina del Mar where we visited the Hotel O'Higgins and witnessed a car crash that ended up with a car turned on its side. As usual with Latin countries no one took any notice and drove around the poor fellow. I stopped the traffic and climbed onto the car pulling the driver clear; there was petrol everywhere but I eventually co-erced some locals into helping me right the car and push it to the side. The driver, now recovered, jumped in and oblivious to the dangers drove away. We spent the evening with Wolfgang drinking Pisco Sour then returned to the ship to sail back to Panama and home as my contract was coming to an end.

I had decided that I was not going to stay in CI as replacement officers were either Sri Lankan or Bangladeshi; British Officers were to be got rid of. I was right, it is normal for the company to fail to inform an officer that he will not be employed at the end of his leave. After three months without pay that is a serious problem and it happened to several of my colleagues. It used to amaze me that companies would expect loyalty yet act with callous efficiency. I tried to reason with a Swedish ship owner's daughter a few years later but it dawned on me that she had no interest in or knowledge of an average seaman's life.

On my return home I started looking for alternative employment; jobs were more numerous than I had expected. The way the others on the ship talked you would think that there was no other company on earth. This is a common attitude in most companies, the idea being that if you move around companies there must be something wrong with you, but this is no longer the case as experienced Seamen of all trades are in short supply.

The first interview was with a company called Low Line and the owner David Grimes. He arrogantly informed me that his company would be thriving when P&O were dust. I promptly headed for Dover to join P&O European Ferries. CI Shipping telephoned me to join a ship; I replied that I had one called the *Pride of Canterbury*. The personnel officer replied that there was no *Pride of Canterbury* in the company. After a second or two the penny must have dropped; of course they were very disappointed and I was berated for my disloyalty.

In 1996 I met the Captain of the *Atlantic Universal* in Port Elizabeth having sailed with him on the *Scirrocco Universal*. There were no British officers on his ship, and the company was renamed London Ship Management, at the same address in London with the same people. His ship had suffered some damage and a Superintendent with extremely bad manners started an argument during my visit. The Captain apologised to me on my ship when he visited me, but I was not impressed.

CHAPTER VIII

Passengers, June 1990 to September 1993

Passengers are a nuisance, frozen chickens are a much easier cargo to carry. People are referred to as WoWo's or walk-on walk-off cargo, and for this reason I try to avoid sailing even as a passenger on a ferry. The catering staff assigned to look after them are usually on short-term contracts with an awful attitude, fawning over passengers whilst at the same time looking down on them.

I joined P&O in June 1990 spending two months on the aging *Pride of Canterbury* before being transferred to the newer *Pride of Dover* built in 1987 in Germany. She had three main engines with three variable-pitch propellers and a service speed of over 20 knots. The company was still suffering from the effect of the sinking of the *Herald of Free Enterprise* and a strike that had left Dover divided. I was amazed by the conditions, a 1 for 1 leave ratio plus holidays, a profit share scheme and cut-price travel: this was a far cry from the deep-sea lifestyle. I was surprised even more by the attitude of the ship's staff who were unable to stop whining about how hard done by they were and what a hard life they had. When I finally left three years later my reasons for leaving were mainly to get away from the incessant whingeing, which accompanied every working day. I had also never encountered so many sick people; ship's staff would regularly not turn up for work, complaining of everything from flu to acute stress. On occasion I would find myself having to cover duties for others because of various supposed ailments and consequently got heartily sick of it.

A motorcycle accident broke my arm and I was off work for five weeks, my only sick leave, which due to the fact that I had not completed my probationary period of 6 months, was not paid.

The *Pride of Dover* annoyed me. During breakfast one morning a rather haughty Captain enquired as to whether I had trouble getting on a British-flagged vessel after serving on a foreign-flagged ship. I replied that I was ex-Royal Navy which was more British than anything he was likely to have served on, and did not go down well. They never understood that I was not impressed by their ersatz RN style.

Every shipping company does at least one thing well – in P&O it was fire drills which were taken seriously. Most shipping companies play lip service to drills but P&O officers, especially ship's engineers, approached the task with diligence. This is an overall comment and obviously attitudes differed according to individual perceptions of what was required. On most occasions I could suggest different ways of approaching problems but some people resented my RN background and could not accept that I had both dealt with fires and instructed on different techniques. This was especially true of the catering department who would insist on shutting all doors and windows around a bomb (during exercises) despite my warning that this would merely concentrate the blast. I advised on opening an escape route for the blast to the upper deck, but I was ignored despite my training and experience, which was annoying.

In 1991 I served on the freight ferries *European Trader* and *European Clearway* and later on the newly built *European Seaway*, *European Pathway* and *European Highway*. I preferred my short visits to the freight ferries, who were friendlier and the newer ships had more interesting equipment to work on.

On the passenger ferries we would work a 13½-hour shift followed by a day off; nights consisted of five or six 10½-hour shifts followed by a week off. On the freighters the rotation was week on, week off, week on, two weeks off. With no Radio Officer I had the navaids to look after, which was no problem as contractors on service agreements looked after most of the equipment. On my second trip on the *Pathway* a Radio Officer joined the ship and I was instructed to teach him the job of ETO. As he was actually on more money than me I resented this, all decisions were made by me and he was of very little help. However I was fair to him, after all it was not his fault. Returning to the *Pride of Dover* was not a happy prospect. On one of my last trips I found that instead of two electrical officers I was by myself, once again sickness having prevailed.

On the first trip to Calais the steering gear failed; with one hour to turn the ship round and 2,000 passengers aboard, I had to work quickly. An inspection of the bridge console soon found a broken wire. Getting a soldering iron I manoeuvred my hands into a small space in order to repair the defect. Suddenly my shoulder was shaken and I turned around to find a stewardess waiving around a broken vacuum cleaner burbling about Captain's rounds. I pointed out that the ship could not depart without steering gear. She brought a Purser and they both started annoying me. Then the Captain entered the bridge demanding to know why I had been stopped, and the Purser was led away. Catering departments now known as hotel services, never understand that their needs are often secondary to the needs of the ship. The ship sailed and I spent the rest of the day chasing problems on several other systems including the elevators.

One incident on the *Pride of Kent* confirmed my opinion of catering staff. I joined to find a former senior Purser with CI working as a steward. I remarked to the Purser on this who sneered that he was just a steward now; he could not see that the tables could so easily have been turned – I had a trade, they generally do not.

When the *European Pathway* came out I was asked to join at short notice, sickness again. The ship immediately blacked out in the engine room three generators had failed due to faulty pressure switches. Switches and transducers on the four main engines were to regularly fail on these ships. Later I changed eighty pressure transducers on one ship alone in three days. At first no one believed that they had failed and I had to endure some criticism before being proved to be correct. Needless to say the ship sailed. The Chief Engineer, Bill Fogarty, has remained a friend ever since. On one occasion a German lorry driver leant on the emergency stop button on an elevator. He panicked, Bill tried to calm him down whilst waiting for me to get him out but in his panic he wrecked the lift car, climbing onto the top of it and kicking out. I had to climb down the lift shaft to free him, as I was unable to wind the car to the next floor in case I caught the German in the winding gear. On seeing me he climbed back into the car and I had to coax him up the ladder to the next deck. Such is the effect of claustrophobia. On leaving the enclosed space he immediately calmed down

During a return to the *Pride of Dover* one Captain could not understand why I preferred freight ships. He referred to them as 'parcels division', in a disparaging way suggesting that people on those ships were somehow inferior. I received more money, worked with good engineers and did not have to put up with the sort of snobbery endemic on P&O passenger ships.

The *Pride of Kent* (sister to the *Herald of Free Enterprise*) had been lengthened in Sicily, and the Palermo shipyard Fincantieri had made a mess of it. I was seconded to a maintenance group dedicated to transforming the ship into something approaching reasonable. I worked under Les Powell a Chief Engineer who I learned to respect. We have not worked together for eight years but I still keep in touch with him. We worked day shifts all week, but had most weekends off except when I was required to stand in as duty electrical officer. Neil Farquhar was one of the Electrical Officers on the ship's staff later being promoted to Senior Electrical Officer then Technical Manager ashore, another extremely able and talented man with a good sense of humour. As the work for the ship decreased the manning of the maintenance unit decreased, and Les left me in charge of four electrical officers and two third engineers. I realised that I would soon be returning to the fleet and after three years started looking for another company. People were amazed that I would leave P&O but I had had enough. In some ways it was as hard to leave as the RN but even after all of the problems I have had over the years I do not regret it. I had moved my family down to Dover after selling our house in Scotland, but I knew that to stay in P&O would be denying myself the variety and experience needed to move on to a better position. I left in June 1993.

My reasons for leaving were incomprehensible to others on the ship, but to me it was very clear. I was not paid in 1990 after my accident despite moving house at great personal expense, the so-called P&O welfare department failing to help me, and I never forgot that difficult time. I was used to sort out the new freight vessels and despite requests from the ship's staff to retain me I was always put back on passenger ferries, which I found to be an inferior job due to the number of people on the ship. The final nail in the coffin was being put in charge of six men without being promoted. It was time to go.

Just before I left there was a union meeting over company proposals to make a Second Officer redundant, which affected several jobs. I later learned that it was a retiring Senior Captain who had suggested it, the extra officer having been employed to take charge on the vehicle deck after the *Herald of Free Enterprise*. The company could say that they were taking advice. I left before the final outcome but officers serving at Dover now work on an offshore agreement with diminished terms and conditions. That a fellow seaman could do this shocked me I could not understand how this man who had such a short time left to serve could indulge in company politics to the detriment of fellow seafarers.

My next position was with V Ships, a company that had its head office in Monaco and an office in Southampton. They had purchased the elderly Dawn Princess from P&O and were currently refitting it in Los Angeles (San Pedro). Built on the Clyde in 1956 for Cunard as the *Sylvania* she was already very old and had originally transported emigrants to Australia, then been converted to a cruise vessel and been renamed the *Fairwind*. She had two steam turbines and steam generators. The next three months were going to be very interesting indeed. Added to the confusion she was called the TSS *Albatros* (German spelling) – not a good omen.

I was employed as Chief Electrician. Being the only Brit on the ship did not worry me (a British Second Engineer had walked off the ship in Los Angeles after a quick walk around). The ship was old, the equipment largely in a poor state of repair, safety devices were shorted out and I faced a lot of hostility from the outgoing Italian Chief Electrician. The electricians were largely Portuguese, their English virtually zero. The First Electrician I inherited knew the ship; altogether there were four of them. This was not enough and six Polish electricians followed by two Indians joined the ship

It soon became apparent that the Italian Chief Electrician (retained to 'help' me) was doing his best to get in my way. He was essentially dishonest and after a week I asked that he be removed from the ship. He left the ship at noon yet put in an overtime claim for that day of eleven hours. I have never been paid overtime; more is expected of British officers. Things improved and the ship had an electrical and safety inspection by the insurers. We got through despite an independent report that slammed the safety drills; in short a lot of the Italian Engineers just could not be bothered. The author of that report now works for V Ships.

We sailed and I soon found that the Polish to my surprise were very dismissive of the Portuguese and Indians; this was ill founded as I found that they themselves were no better and in some aspects inferior to the other two nationalities. After a week I found out that all was not well, which was highlighted by a problem with the after sewage treatment plant. I was called to the bridge where I found that all power had been switched off and the Captain was not happy. The Polish First Electrician had turned off power to the sewage plant but it was still being supplied. The Italian Captain and Chief Engineer clubbed together to give me a hard time; it was clear that arguing on the bridge was not going to sort this problem out so I made my excuses and left. I called the Portuguese First Electrician and after a short lecture on safety he admitted that the outgoing Italian had changed over the labels on the power and distribution switchboard. The power to the bridge was restored ten minutes after I left the bridge. The knowledge that a fellow Italian had committed such a terrible crime silenced the others, although it was simply forgotten, and true to type they found other things to complain about. We now had suspicion and underlying distrust as we headed for Panama where we encountered new problems.

Too much had been expected of my largely poorly trained electricians. The Portuguese First Electrician, due to an accident on the same ship three years earlier, had terrible burns across his face. I wanted to avoid similar accidents and had outlawed certain practices, which were extremely dangerous. During a particularly busy time in Panama with equipment failing I was tasked with moving the Casino to a different location, enlarging one of the restaurants and installing power supplies, installing 200 televisions, dealing with generator problems, repairing several defective motors and installing transformers for the new computerised tills in the bars and shops. The ship blacked out I soon traced this to a sub-station where a Polish electrician doing precisely what I had told him not to do was blinded and burnt after a near fatal accident. He was sent to hospital and I was one man down but after fifty-two hours without sleep we sailed. Half an hour after retiring I was called out to swap loads on a generator. I was then called to the hospital where I fell asleep, when I awoke I had been undressed and put to bed by the Doctor.

We arrived in Lisbon for our passenger certificate, which we obtained. It was here that I learnt that fifteen days after the agreed payment date I had not been paid. After my performance I was insulted, my wife was getting letters from our mortgage company asking for more money and we also incurred bank charges. I rebelled, but the company did not understand. My pay was late in June, they apologised, and it was late again in July, so I complained and went on strike. In August it was late again, and this time managers in Monaco telephoned my wife to tell her to be quiet as she was upsetting me. This really annoyed me, if they had just stuck to the contract between us all would have been well. Finally in September I gave up, as did the German Doctor, twenty Austrian stewards and stewardesses, the Anglo-German Chief Cook, the Italian maître'D and an Italian first engineer. We all left in Kiel; they tried to make me pay my own way but in the end paid my costs and flight along with all back pay. They had little choice, we were on our second cruise in the Norwegian Fjords and were embarking passengers, threatening them with a demonstration on the jetty.

To dwell on the negative aspects of this voyage would be to ignore the many positive points. To begin with I learnt a lot about people, I was never good at languages but soon developed a large Italian vocabulary. We visited beautiful Norwegian fjords and saw blue glaciers in stunning scenery. Ports visited included Hammerfest, Nordkapp, Andalsnes, Tromso, Bergen, Gothenberg, Copenhagen and Bremerhaven. When I managed to get into the passenger spaces in my Italian-designed, American-style uniform (resembling a South American admiral's) I did relax. It was a pity that money spent on the passenger accommodation was not matched in the engine room. In reality the ship which later dry-docked in Genoa should have been completely refitted before embarking passengers. The ship itself was well built and must have been improved greatly as in 2001 she is still trading; I last saw her in Bremerhaven in September 1999.

My knowledge of shipping companies has put me off choosing a cruise for my own holiday, the last time I crossed the English Channel I chose to travel through the tunnel, which was quicker, and I did not have to put up with surly stewards and haughty pursers. Ships can be poorly maintained and the crew disgruntled over low pay and poor conditions. On the *Albatros* there were too many nationalities – for example in the crew accommodation the official language was English, but there were only two out of 300 who spoke it as a first language. In the passenger spaces the official language was German due to having German passengers. Communication was hopeless, even the three radio officers had problems, one being German, another Dutch and the third one Polish. The Italians spoke neither language well, resented having to and regularly misinterpreted my intentions; the Philippinos spoke English well. We had British, Italian, German, Portuguese, Polish, Dutch, Danish, Indian,

Philippino, Indonesian, South African, Brazilian and one Thai crew member. A veritable tower of Babel and it is as well that we did not encounter a serious disaster.

The ship ran aground in 1998; the company blamed Trinity House for moving a buoy, which was highly unlikely and not proved. She was repaired and I was informed on 7 June 2001 by the magazine *Ships Monthly* that she is still in service.

From 1993 to 1997 I served with P&O and Stena Line on various ferries including the *Norsky, Stena Invicta, Stena Challenger* and *Stena Empereur* on short-term fill-in jobs between leaves whilst working for other companies. This to make money to support Gwen in her quest to obtain a BSc honours degree and my now growing sons.

Passenger ships changed my perspective on life and work, where companies deserve to be treated ruthlessly, colleagues with suspicion. It took me some time to come to terms with this view as I have always tried to be loyal, but it is a misplaced loyalty.

Two incidents on the *Stena Invicta* hardened my attitude. On my first day I witnessed an accident whilst hoisting a lifeboat. The Chief Officer froze, I shouted to stop and the winch stopped; had I not acted eleven people in the boat may have been thrown from it. As it was they all got out alive. In the enquiry the Chief Officer blamed me for his own shortcomings. I was asked if I needed a friend to accompany me into the enquiry, but I said no. The Chief Officer was disciplined while I was thanked for my quick intervention. After three weeks I was due to go back to my deep-sea job. I had already stated that I wanted to go home every night unlike everyone else who lived on-board. The company agreed, although the other two electricians complained. Finally I left the ship, but I was recalled due to a blackout and I negotiated another day's pay. The ship sailed, and I went home.

In November 1997 I served on my last passenger ferry which lasted for three weeks before joining a container ship, I have no intention of sailing on another. My present employment has meant that I have taken ferries from Le Havre to Portsmouth and Harwich to Hamburg as a passenger but in general I try to avoid it.

CHAPTER IX

Snow Boats and Sweden

After the trouble on the *Albatros* I had to get a job quickly and so I phoned the many agencies who put sailors and companies together. Blue Star called me to London for interview; I needed money. The interview lasted two hours with a lot of stupid questions; if they had asked me to suggest ways of saving money I could have suggested the redundancy of several in the office. Eventually I ran out of patience and got up to walk out, saying, 'If you want to employ me go ahead if not please do not waste my time.' They gave me the job of Electrical Officer on the *Canterbury Star*, a reefer. I joined it on 29 September 1993 for a short-term two-month contract.

Joining the ship in Zeebrugge I soon found myself up the mast with the Electrical Superintendent fitting a new radar.

The *Canterbury Star* was built in Harland and Wolf, Belfast in 1986 and symbolised the demise of British shipbuilding. At 19 knots she was too slow for the 20-knot charter she was on; in bad weather she slowed to a near stop, vibrated too much and was an extremely uncomfortable ship to be on. She had four hatches with four cranes, the cranes being of a poor Clarke Chapman design. The alarm plant was a Richwest, also unreliable and prone to failure. We were trading from Zeebrugge to Santa Marta in Columbia, Moin in Costa Rica then back across the Atlantic to Zeebrugge with a cargo of bananas.

This was not the most miserable ship I have ever been on, but it came close. There were only three British on board, the Captain, Chief Engineer and myself. The term of two months was extended to three months two weeks and I thought it would never end. Christmas day epitomised Blue Star – the Captain pandered to the Philippino crew, who had suckling pig as per tradition on Christmas Eve; on Christmas day we had sandwiches. The company would buy one can of beer for all Blue Star employees, but as the Captain and myself were working for

Austasia Line the only one eligible was the Chief Engineer. The Captain had no imagination at all; we were even weather-routed by people ashore to keep us out of rough weather. In the winter to go via the great north circle, whilst being the shortest route, is not the best when you know that your ship slows to a near stop. Instead of going south he went north, the weather was terrible and once again we were late. It was no surprise to me that Blue Star lost the charter after one year. I have since sailed with captains who do know their business and make their decisions based on knowledge.

On 8 December 1993, we were in Moin; everyone went ashore and I returned early. The fire alarms went off, I went to my station and the Philippino Officers just looked at me not knowing what to do. I calmed them down, organised a search and soon found that it was a false alarm. The Electrical Superintendent thanked me for my work. I had improved the cranes but I knew the job was temporary; to be honest I could not wait to get off. I departed in Zeebrugge in January 1993. Going back on ferries was terrible but I endured the *Stena Challenger* from March to April 1994.

A few other jobs presented themselves, including Bibby Line who offered me really low wages to work on the *Baltic Eider* from Felixstowe

MV Snow Crystal

to the Baltic ports. One week before I was due to join the *Baltic Eider* a Swedish company was given my telephone number by one of the agencies. I subsequently worked for this company for three years from May 1994 to March 1997, occasionally doing some ferry work as well to support my family and particularly Gwen who was starting her studies which she has since completed, never before or since have I earned so much money or been so long away.

The company was called Norman International when I joined it but this was changed to Holy House Shipping by the owner. He was called Matts Ruhne and was, to say the least, a little eccentric but enormous fun and the most ruthless man I have ever met. Matts, this chapter is for you.

The *Snow Crystal* was in Antwerp where I joined it on 5 May 1994 with a new Second Engineer, Mark Rush. On the ship already was Christoph Goehler, a German Chief Engineer who I have now sailed with on a number of occasions. The Captain, Andy Hamill, was a real live wire from western Scotland and despite the hard work those people were a pleasure to sail with.

There were eight ships in the class all built in the early 1970s and Matts owned three, *Snow Crystal, Snow Flower* and *Snow Drift*. I had

First Engineer John Hagan, with me (on right), MV Snow Crystal

From Left: Cristoph Goehler (Chief Engineer); Myself (Electronics Officer); Mark Rush (First Engineer). MV Snow Crystal Control Room

My son David (on left) and Bosun, Rudy Sarmiento, MV Snow Crystal

the good fortune to sail on all three. They had five refrigerated hatches with eight cranes making them very versatile ships. We were taking apples, grapes and plums from Capetown to Europe. As the season progressed we started taking oranges from Durban to Europe. After the fruit season was over we would tramp around taking any and all kinds of cargo from cars to frozen chickens, bananas and on one occasion large drums of orange juice. During that first trip we called at Capetown, Durban, Antwerp, Sheerness, Le Havre and finally Tilbury.

She was showing signs of age and we had a few problems with the generator switchboard and most of all the data logger. This is very important on a reefer because it records the temperatures around the hatches and is the only proof you have in the event of a damaged cargo claim from the receivers of that cargo. Somehow we managed to keep it going with the help of one ex-IBM teleprinter engineer who would take defective printers off and service them. Unfortunately they tended to go wrong when we were at sea and I had a busy time trying to sort them out.

Capetown was excellent, Christoph, Mark and myself went ashore and soon made friends with the agency who looked after us. I must thank Rob André and Danie Wiese for making our visits to Capetown memorable and on occasions bordering on wild. One bar we went in was particularly dark, and I could not see very well. Christoph spoke up, 'I think we are in the wrong place, all the men are kissing each other.' Needless to say we left.

The turnaround in the port taking on a complete cargo was twenty-four hours; three years later we were spending weeks instead of days. This was fine by us but no good for the South African economy, which has suffered from the need to replace white workers with black. I understand the argument and the need, but it should have happened slower. Half-trained crane drivers started putting dents in the ship, which sustained some damage. It was mostly superficial, but there was a definite slow down.

On one occasion in 1995 we loaded oranges in Durban, and the stevedores went on strike over taxes. We sailed to Capetown and spent a wonderful two weeks, parties were attended with our ever-growing list of friends and we even went on a wine tour of the Stellenbosch region, from which I have acquired a taste for nice wines.

I left the *Snow Crystal* in August 1994 joining the *Snow Flower* in

Falmouth dry dock in September. I was disappointed – this was one of the unhappiest ships I have ever joined. The Captain was a misery. When he refused permission for the Second Engineers Brazilian wife to sail with us (she had been living on the ship for two weeks) there was a lot of bad feeling.

We sailed from Falmouth to Miami where we loaded used cars; we then transited the Panama Canal and went to Callao in Peru. The 2nd Engineer and myself went ashore and soon found it to be very unfriendly. We ended up in a karaoke bar with a load of Japanese fishermen trying to sing Beetles favourites before falling down. I was happy to get back to the ship. A young Swede who was sailing with us was robbed of his trainers, we warned him about going ashore alone, but he did not listen any more than he did to the warning about staying in the sun too long. He was in some pain for a time but he never seemed to learn from his mistakes and gave us constant amusement. In Guyacquil in Ecuador he fell in love with a girl who had several sisters all the same age. I even had to translate letters for him, but he would not listen to any warnings: love is blind.

In Ecuador we loaded bananas, suffering a plague of small black rats that seemed to be everywhere. The Philippino crew chased them all over the place and I was surprised that we never saw them again as I was sure that we would have some unwelcome stowaways.

We also went to Iquique and Valporaiso where we once again met Wolfgang in the Hamburg Restaurant. The Second Engineer was now in a really bad mood, so I took him ashore. The repair firm we used let him telephone home free, Wolfgang gave us a tankard each and a load of free beer, but he was still miserable. We did not see him for two days which put a lot of strain on the rest of us. He resigned and we left bound for Buenos Aires.

BA was a delight at first. Branko a Yugoslav (from Montenegro) had joined to replace the Second Engineer and we went ashore. We had trouble with a bar that tried to charge us $100 for two drinks, which we just managed to deal with. Then we went for a meal where I used my credit card. About two months later a bill arrived at my house for several thousand pounds apparently from a furniture store. I managed to prove that I had not lost my card and had been at sea when it was supposed to have been used. I was refunded.

After our trip ashore in BA the taxi driver could not find the ship

MV Snow Drift

and an argument ensued. I went to the police station and for 200 cigarettes managed to get a lift back to the ship; Branko walked.

From BA we went on to Santos in Brazil where the Second Engineer paid off; we were all relieved as his misery was transmitted to us all. The Captain was as obnoxious as ever. He used to get promotional gifts from sales reps, T-shirts, lighters etc. One shirt he wore without washing for at least a week. Branko told him that the camel on the front would soon start talking. Another annoying habit he had was continually picking his nose, stating that people who picked their nose live ten years longer. I have never sailed with this creature since and hope I never will.

In Rotterdam the owner visited us and the Captain was relieved by Bill Lockie. He had a fearsome reputation but I found him to be mostly harmless; being extremely loud and excitable did not endear him to people but I found him to be quite tame. Christmas 1994 was spent in Canaveral, where we were amused when an American taxi driver asked Branko if Montenegro was near London. Being an American he knew little of the outside world; they can be an extremely insular race. As Americans were involved in the region at the time you would expect them to take a little more interest.

ENSIGNS AND ECHOES

We loaded frozen chickens in Canaveral for Capetown, and it was here that I realised that the Captain was all talk. We had to land a large motor for repair and needed one of the ship's cranes to do it. I asked the stevedore Foreman who told me there would be no cargo for twenty minutes. We offloaded the motor in ten. Later that evening the Captain complained that he had been fined $2,000 for stoppage of cargo time. I wrote a letter to complain and the company was reimbursed. He had accepted the word of the shore authorities without a fight; he even asked me if 'I really wanted to send that letter'. That people he had sailed with were scared of him made me laugh – he was just an old man doing his job in the best way he could, but a disciplinarian he was not.

In Capetown the owner came with a container full of motorcycles and a lot of business friends. They stayed on the ship as we were in port for some time due to the slow discharge of the cargo. One evening I posed for my photograph on a 650cc Moto Guzzi. The Captain got on the back not knowing I had the keys. I started the motor and raced up and down the quayside with Bill shouting in my ear, 'Put your hands back on the handlebars.' I replied that I was the Captain of this ship and he should behave himself. We had a good laugh; the owner leant me his 750cc Triumph Trident the next day and with two Swedes on Indians we hurtled off down to Simonstown where Granddad's old ship had just been laid to rest. The coast road was very scenic and the Swedes hung off their bikes to take photographs at 40 m.p.h., which scared the life out of me. We saw a lot of seals and penguins and came back on the main road. Then we stowed the bikes in the containers and got on with the more mundane rituals involved in cooling down to take on apples.

The cargo discharge continued with an amusing incident at two o'clock one morning. There was a chicken disease in South Africa, which was why we were there with a cargo of chickens. The refrigerated trucks had armed guards on, as there had been some hijacking going on. The police had found a man selling chickens illegally. They actually brought the chicken back to the ship, awoke the Captain and asked him if this was one of his. With thousands of chickens on board this was a foolish question. I believe he answered in the affirmative.

After two days at sea we found a stowaway, a young man who was kept on the ship under lock and key. This was for his own safety as it is not unknown for stowaways when caught to jump over the side to

Capetown 1995, Captain Bill Lockie and I on a 650cc Moto Guzzi Motorcycle

Me on motorcycle, Snow Flower behind, 1995

certain death. He told me he came from Rwanda but it turned out he was lying. He was taken off the ship in Germany for two days then returned. I last saw him in Sheerness; he eventually left the ship in South Africa back where he started from. His intention was to get to Canada; I often wonder whether he ever made it.

I left the ship in February 1995 in Sheerness, not my favourite place but after five months away I was glad to be home. I did not expect to return so I started to do temporary jobs on ferries as mentioned in the last chapter. In April I was asked to join the *Snow Crystal* again in Sheerness on 1 May.

I rejoined the *Snow Crystal*, a Scottish Chief Engineer was on board with his American girlfriend as was a particularly mad South African Second Engineer who had reportedly been in the South African army in a very active unit. The Chief Engineer was a Christian who did not drink or smoke and spent his leave on the *Anastasia*, an aging cruise ship that would call in at African ports dispensing medicine and Christianity in equal amounts. We heard much of this vessel and were highly amused when it was threatened with arrest in Capetown for non-payment of bills. On that occasion we hosted a party for the South African farmers. The Chief was ashore with his girlfriend leaving the Captain, Second Engineer and myself to entertain them. During the party, which we attended in uniform, there was a blackout, so John (the Second) and myself went below, sorted the problem and returned. The farmers just continued drinking as if nothing had happened. The Chief came back and announced that he had just proposed to the girlfriend.

We went back and forward from Antwerp to Capetown, then Port Elizabeth and Durban. On one trip we ferried Stefan Richter, son of a fruit importer in Germany. He was an excellent fellow who offered to help me and soon became very useful on deck and a good companion in the bar. Christoph asked me to stay on to sort out the data logger and I was asked to fit the new GMDSS radio satellite distress system, which would eliminate the need for the Radio Officer. Peter Bergholtz, the Manager for Furuno Sweden, came on to finish it off. Peter left the ship in Gdansk in Poland.

When the ship was built it was designed to run with thirty-six Officers and crew; after the RO was taken off we were down to a British Captain, German Chief Engineer, British Electronics Officer and Second Engineer and fifteen Philippinos, nineteen men in total. The ship was harder to run due to its age, but the owner told me that he would never find a Swede to work under those terms and conditions. I think that times have changed and the cotton wool wrapping has come off Swedish officer's contracts as they emerge into the real world where we all compete on the same market. There were plenty of cabins for Matts to entertain his millionaire friends.

It was now 10 October 1995; after five months I needed some leave. After taking my wife to Paris for a weekend (Hovercraft, awful experience) I came home to find messages from the company asking me to get in touch. They had told one of the electronic officers that he was not required for five months. This is a long time without pay so he got a job ashore to last him. At the last minute they were shocked to be told no when they asked him to return. They moaned to me about his disloyalty and were not amused when I pointed out that they were not paying him so why should he wait for them. The moaning stopped and I was asked to go to Gdynia in Poland to inspect the vessel they had recently purchased and find out why the control system (early electronic) was not working. I had been home three weeks but needing the money off I went.

The ship was called the *Clementina* and had arrived in Poland with a cargo of bananas. The company sent me by the cheapest air route, Heathrow to Brussels with Sabena, SAS to Copenhagen then LOT to Gdansk. It was no wonder that my bags ended up in Warsaw and I did not see them for several days. They had to be collected from an open cart in a snowstorm.

The ship was in a terrible mess, the crew were Burmese, the Captain and First Mate were Polish and the Chief Engineer was Lithuanian. In the course of the next three weeks I found that nearly every safety device on compressors and the main engine were out of order and shorted out. The engine when ordered ahead sometimes refused to start or would go astern. The engine room was black and very little worked, maintenance was nil. The radio station also did not work and as I inspected everything from the bridge to the engine room I realised that this would be a long job.

By the time I left in Cristobal, Panama the main engine worked as did the data logger and some of the radio station. I had spent three weeks in terrible conditions; in the crew mess the TV and bulkheads were spattered with little dots, caused by the crew spitting after chewing beetle nuts; they were the dirtiest crew I have ever seen as well as the laziest. The Polish Chief Engineer who replaced the Lithuanian was very good but the job was too much for one man, the ship had fallen into too serious a condition. He fell over in the engine room as some deck plates had been removed; it was so dirty that it was hard to distinguish between the bilge and the plates. His leg was badly gashed and when the company ordered me to attend another ship I felt bad about leaving him with this ghastly crew.

The ship I had to join was the *Snow Drift*, which was discharging plastic fulminate in Koh Si Chang in Thailand. I was taken by taxi through what seemed like jungle from *Cristobal* to Panama City. A nightmare ride in a car that kept braking down, cigarettes were handed out to the customs officials and off we went. I never saw the *Clementina* again.

A sleepless few hours were spent in a tiny hotel and at 0130 hrs I was picked up to go to the airport. The customs tried to charge me $50 departure tax but with the help of the agent it was reduced to $20, then after some argument he paid. Flying Lloyd Aero Boliviano to Mexico was an experience; the stewardess put me in business class, just as well judging from the noise coming from behind. She told me I would have trouble in Mexico City Airport, I asked why and she replied, 'Because we do.' I behaved despite being searched three times, filling in dozens of forms and being sent to wait in countless queues. In the end I just emptied my bags on the floor in desperation, they laughed and left me to repack. And I was only transiting – what would have happened if I wanted to enter the country can only be imagined.

The next flight took me to Los Angeles with United Airways; my company always found the cheapest way and UA must have been very cheap. Seldom have I been as uncomfortable on a flight. Due to a security exercise I had to pick my baggage up and lug it across LA airport, by which time I was extremely tired. The flight to Hong Kong was delayed by several hours and I missed my connection to Bangkok. The next night was spent in a hotel courtesy of UA who could not understand that my ship might not be around when I arrived in Koh Si Chang, I gave up trying to explain.

There are people who cannot understand that ships move. I have encountered this phenomenon on several occasions; these people are usually intelligent and it is hard to see where their logic comes from.

One man could not understand that I did not have a base port; the company was based in Sweden yet the ships did not go there once whilst I was on board. An electrical supplier whose order had been delayed still wanted to send the equipment to the port the ship had been in despite the fact that he knew the ship had sailed. The conclusion I have reached is that people fail to understand that a ship is self-supporting – most make their own fresh water from seawater, fuel oil can be obtained in almost every port, as can food, toilet rolls, spares, tools, paper (for the ever hungry computers) and all manner of other items. When a ship catches fire at sea it is usually put out by the officers and crew, as in mid Pacific or Atlantic even in these days it is still a very lonely place. Ships make their own electricity and can communicate through satellite, they do not stop at night and due to the fact that they do not stop cover vast distances in short times. Capetown to Antwerp with full cargo could be accomplished in under two weeks on a *Snow* without stopping.

There was no one to meet me in Bangkok Airport; a call to the company confirmed that I was to wait for the Captain's wife and their twelve-year-old daughter. They arrived with no luggage and the mother had been overimbibing. I will not describe the shopping trip to buy new clothes and other things in Bangkok or the nightmare journey to KSC which was around 120 kilometres, the memory is too painful. At KSC I found that the ship was at anchor discharging into barges. We had to jump across broken concrete piles over what used to be a jetty; it was dark and people were running around everywhere, not a pleasant experience when accompanied by a mother and daughter who had to be transported to the ship. I took their bags and helped them onto the boat. When we got alongside the ship I had to push the twelve-year-old girl onto the ladder, as she was afraid to jump from the boat to the ship. We got on board where the Swedish Superintendent wanted a full report from me as he had waited to see me especially.

The next day the luggage arrived for the Captain's wife, which included Christmas presents for the daughter; we were all very relieved.

The ship sailed for Capetown and as we arrived early we expected to stay at anchor. Luckily the owner paid for us to go alongside on the understanding that we used the time to good effect.

On Christmas Day, not wishing to intrude on the others as they all had their wives with them, I decided to climb Table Mountain from the ship to the top without the use of the cable car. It was an excellent day.

Table Mountain, 1996

I saw snakes and Rock Dacies (Hyrax) on the way up and although the day started off foggy, as I got nearer the top the weather got better and I was treated to a wonderful view. I had Christmas dinner of fish and chips in the restaurant at the top with an Englishman who had taken time off work and was following the England cricket team around the world. The return trip was made in the cable car.

We left Capetown and resumed the regular run to Antwerp and Sheerness. Antwerp is a favourite port of mine as Dirk Daems (who had been the ship's agent) regularly visited us and we had some great parties. Dirk will go down in history as having the dirtiest jokes I have ever heard. He spends his spare time as a disc jockey at charity events and revels in the name of Dirty Dirk.

Whilst on the *Snow Drift* I was asked to suggest a solution to the data logger problem on the *Snow Crystal*, so I made notes and sent telex and on my return home I proposed to my family that we all go to Sweden. My wife drove all the way; we crossed the channel from Ramsgate to Ostende then drove through Europe to Denmark, catching the ferry at Frederikshaven to Gothenberg where we were met at 0200 by a tired Peter Bergholtz.

SNOW BOATS AND SWEDEN

We stayed with Peter for a few excellent days. Peter took us up in a light aircraft and we over flew Gothenberg harbour and Peter's house. At one point David my eldest son took the controls (he had been flying with the Air Training Corps in Chipmunks) and we all had a scary time. Peter was ex-Swedish Navy having served on an ice breaker. We looked through his old photographs and with good accommodation and an air of relaxed comfort it made me realise that this was a far cry from the cramped conditions of a RN warship. They also had long hair and I was instantly extremely jealous.

March in Sweden was amazing, ice on the sea yet warm enough to have a barbecue. Later we ate at a restaurant called Rakans. They put prawns in radio-controlled model fishing boats and we had to pilot our own boat across the water in the middle of the restaurant. Peter arranged for me to be given a fishing skippers licence (only valid in the restaurant) which was really for children.

After a few days we went on to Stockholm, were duly installed in a hotel and after being wined and dined visited the office the next day. Matts as usual was eccentric in a pair of multi-coloured spectacles. My eldest son was on holiday from college in the summer and I asked Matts if he could take David on as a temporary apprentice for six weeks. He said yes and David carried on the tradition of travelling. We had been offered a place to stay in Matts's summerhouse but as there was a metre of permafrost the water pipes were frozen. We were driven there by Anna his daughter and the setting next to a lake on a frozen sunny day was idyllic. This was now the end of March 1996; I had exactly one year left in the company.

David joined the ship in Bremen and started work. We had a particularly anti-social Second Engineer from Hull who did nothing but moan. However David and I had a great time calling at Saldanha Bay where we once again met Rob André and had a nice meal. After that we called at Port Elizabeth and Durban where we visited the snake and crocodile centre. This was particularly memorable as we were allowed to handle a poisonous snake (under supervision), something I could not imagine happening in England. David suffered badly from the heat, which in the engine room was intense due to the failure of the fan casings, as they were rotten.

We sailed back to Antwerp where we had a night out with the famous Dirk Daems and then to Southampton where my son left.

ENSIGNS AND ECHOES

The Second Engineer had a problem when he overheard Christoph and myself talking about a strange man, and thought we were talking about him. Actually I was explaining that the author of a book I had just read had some funny ideas. This is mentioned because it highlights the result of long periods of isolation. The Second was suffering from paranoia and after we had a conversation about this he soon told me of a number of problems he was experiencing – he thought the other officers were all talking about him which was all in his imagination. That was the last time I sailed with him, since when a number of other people have asked me of his whereabouts but he seems to have disappeared. He was married to a girl in Brazil so I can only surmise that he has gone to live there.

I left the ship in October 1996 and went on leave. In December I was asked to pick up some paperwork for the ship and join the *Snow Drift* in Yokohama. I flew from Heathrow to Frankfurt then on to Narita airport, which serves Tokyo. We flew in on a clear day but I noticed a layer of smog over the city; on landing I noticed that most people wore masks the pollution was so bad. The trip to Yokohama took about an hour and a half through an industrial wasteland presided over by large

Capetown Drydock

structures of steel and glass, a most unpleasant place that I never wish to return to.

The ship loaded second-hand cars in Yokohama and Nagoya then sailed to Durban where we discharged them to be forwarded to Tanzania. The *Snow Drift* was due to go to dry dock and we sailed to Capetown.

The dry dock in Capetown went fairly well, but the workforce had to be closely watched as they would find any excuse not to do a job well and would skive off. The manager tried to buy me off with a bottle of whiskey but I was not tempted.

One Sunday Danie Wiese from the agency asked me if I wanted to climb Table Mountain from the back. This was a most exhilarating climb, which reduced me to a sweaty mess. There were huge tadpoles in the streams (and bigger frogs) brightly coloured butterflies and iridescent lizards. The view was particularly awe-inspiring as I looked down on the Lions Head, which I had been standing under only two hours before. Deep ravines cut into the back of the mountain and some paths were closed off due to falling rocks, it is a very dramatic landscape.

As the dock flooded we were running machinery up, the ship left the dock, went across to the loading berth and immediately started loading cargo. The first few days at sea were interesting. In one day we suffered a generator failure and a SAT C aerial failure; from the engine room I found myself up the mast with the Captain, soldering iron in hand repairing a faulty cable connection. Things soon settled down and the rest of the trip was uneventful; we arrived in Antwerp ahead of time. After discharging the cargo (plums) we moved to another berth and started loading second-hand and damaged cars. Dirk took us to his village to witness the annual 'Goose riding fair' which turned out to be a competition between three villages with young men riding around on horses trying to snatch a dead goose from a pole. A lot of Belgian beer was drunk including one brew called Duvel, which is particularly potent.

Tadeusz Misiuro had joined the ship as Chief Officer; he had been on the *Clementina*, a large quiet man who has become a good friend over the years. He is now a captain and I wish him good luck.

That voyage from Antwerp to Cotonou was particularly bad – in a storm our anchor became unshipped, and cars on the upper deck were thrown around. One wave crashing down destroyed several cars just by the sheer weight. We were attached to the seabed off Ushant and it took several hours to pull the anchor back up. Our other problem was the

Climbing Table Mountain, Lions Head from above

Me underneath the Lion's Head

Tadeusz Misiuro, Chief Officer, MV Snow Drift

Philippino crew who would go into the hatches and start cars up. With petrol fumes and hot exhausts this was an extremely dangerous thing to do. On one occasion I ordered the Bosun to stop his men from doing this, he attacked me and I swiftly marched him to the Captain. The Chief Engineer witnessed the whole thing but the Captain was unwilling to put the man in the log book and I had to insist. I immediately decided to leave the company; with captains regularly refusing to back up their officers there was no point in carrying on. We docked at Cotonou discharging broken cars by night.

The next port was Paranagua, the evaporator was not working well and as I had visited that port many times I warned that we might stay at anchor for many days; we did. However I could not convince the Captain to stop his men washing down the upper deck with fresh water. The result was water rationing and I became more frustrated.

After Paranagua I resigned, we called in at Durban and I eventually left the ship in Sharjah in the UAE. I had had some good times on the *Snows* but you always know when it is time to leave. After leaving Christoph wrote to me and informed me that Matts had won a court case over a cargo claim and bought another *Snow* ship. More of the same, he had also bought a newer reefer from Lauretzens a Danish company but having served on seven reefers I needed a change. I wish them all well.

I flew home via Qatar with Gulf Air and was pleasantly surprised, as it was an excellent flight.

CHAPTER X

Container Boats, Germans and India

WHEN I RETURNED HOME in March 1997 I was not a well man. The effects of dehydration and dissatisfaction combined to make me extremely unhappy. I started pestering the agencies and eventually I got an interview in Southampton with the British end of a German company based in Cyprus. They manned the *Saga Rose*, an elderly cruise ship but had had a lot of problems with it. I was taken to the ship in Southampton to meet a Chief Engineer who had sailed on the container ship that I was being interviewed to join. There was embarrassment as, when we visited the ship, a crew member was being loaded into an ambulance and fire engines surrounded the ship. She had experienced a number of fires and at one point the crew were suspected of deliberately setting the ship on fire. I suspect that fires were caused by electrical defects, as I know of at least one Electrical Officer who had walked off the ship due to its condition.

Needless to say I was engaged to join the MV *APL China*, a 64,000 tonne, 5,200 TEU container vessel in Hong Kong. She had eight hatches and a single eleven-cylinder MAN/B&W main engine with a service speed of 24.6 knots. APL stood for American President Lines and our company was tasked with the manning and management. She was on a regular run that took her from Hong Kong to Yantian, Singapore, Port Kelang then back to Singapore, Yantian and Hong Kong, followed by a dash across the Pacific to San Pedro (Los Angeles), Seattle then back to Hong Kong. Trips were of four-month duration and in this time the ship would complete three voyages as above.

I relieved the biggest German I ever saw, he was obese and could not get into half of the spaces that he needed to get into.

The German Chief and First Engineer gave me a hard time – they were bigoted, self-opinionated and rude. I was informed on my first day that Englishmen did not last long on this ship, but I completed all my

San Pedro, Los Angeles 1997, Container Port. Taken from Bridge Wing of the ship (note the height)

trips and found that the reason for their rudeness was to hide their lack of knowledge of the ship. I cannot remember how many times I was apologised to. On one occasion the steering gear failed, I was dismissed but stayed around, the Chief Engineer telling me he was fully trained and I was not required. Time passed and he eventually turned to me with a look of pleading. I fixed it in half an hour, found a design fault, corrected it, entered it on a drawing and duly presented the drawing to the company with an explanation of why. This annoying sequence was repeated on a number of occasions with the final straw being when the First Engineer shouted at me because the Chief had switched the boiler to another mode and I was accused. I called the big idiot from Leipzig over and whispered in his ear that if he did not shut up I would put his head down a toilet and flush. There were no more problems, with him.

The Captain was sixty-one years old, a real eccentric who could wreck a piece of bridge Electronic equipment at a glance. The ship had been built in 1995 and had the latest equipment from Sperry put on the ship as a test bed. On my first week he destroyed a printer by feeding paper in the wrong way, then he used to put oil in everything, his maintenance as he called it; this included a laser jet printer which expired and various switches which would burn out. He was a real menace and I often wondered about his sanity. He would order the ship's stores including pig's neck (*schwein nacke*), which he would mash up with potatoes and fish before noisily gulping the foul concoction down. His daughter and her husband joined in Hong Kong and I was amazed to see all three of them devour large quantities of food. The new First Engineer, Jurgan Eng, had joined and proved to be a lot better. During one meal the noise was so bad we both left the table. The daughter informed me that she did not wish to go ashore in Singapore because she had been before and it was boring; this also went for Hong Kong. She was easily the most ignorant person I have ever met at sea.

Drinking was frowned upon but the Germans would take a bottle, lock themselves in their cabins and drink. On a sister ship a German captain argued with the pilot coming out of Seattle, which developed into a heated exchange that resulted in the Chief Officer having to step between them. The pilot ordered the ship back in and it was duly arrested. Some of the captains had been with the company a long time and were moved on to other ships, which would be immediate dismissal for the other nationalities employed.

In the end the Captain was replaced by Captain Frank Brossman, an extremely able and sensible man who I wished had been there from the start. Jurgan the First Engineer informed me two months after I left the ship that the Chief Engineer had told everyone how good I was; he certainly gave me a good report. I have no idea why we had to go all through the unnecessary unpleasantness. On one occasion he berated me in front of his fourteen-year-old son who had joined his father for a few weeks. I remained silent knowing that he did not have the full picture; later on he apologised and I helped him fix a mechanical problem.

While all this was going on my eldest son David signed on as an Engineering Officer Cadet with Trinity House. He went up to South Shields Nautical College in September; another member of the family had decided to go to sea.

Jurgan was an especially interesting man; he had originated in East Germany and under communist rule had served his time on the Berlin Wall. Later he was in the Navy manning boats along the river. He walked near a fence on one occasion which divided East from West, heard a click and looked around to see his officer with a pistol levelled at him. Nothing was said and Jurgan went back. He told me a lot about the East and how corrupt the communist regime was – a commissar on a ship in the lowliest of positions had infinitely more power than the Captain and abuse was common. Jurgan has daughters and when one of them brought home a young man who started a speech on how things should return to the communist way, Jurgan quickly corrected him. Every year Jurgan drives a truck to a small town in Russia with food and supplies. He tells me that parts of Russia are not unlike Ethiopia, starving children with distended bellies; he is perhaps the kindest man I know.

The Chief Officer was replaced by another East German called Benito Klein, who confirmed Jurgans stories of the old East. We often joked that if world war had broken out in the 1970s we would most likely have been shooting at each other. This revelation was followed by bouts of silence as each of us contemplated the awful truth and the result of politicians failing to preserve peace. It is not a new phenomenon – in 1914 Von Spee's squadron of warships had welcomed the Royal Navy into their base at Tsingtao and embarked on a series of parties, regattas and social events. By the end of 1914 Von Spee's squadron, his sons and himself were all dead having been sunk by the very men who they had befriended.

I left the ship in Hong Kong and returned home for two months leave. The company contacted me and asked me to join the MV *Tiger Cape*, a feeder container ship considerably smaller than the one I had been on. The company lost the contract to man and manage the APL ships and whilst I thought them to be very good they did have a serious vibration fault. In the steering gear compartment at full speed the vibration was intolerable, motor mountings and light fittings would crack, hydraulic lines would fracture and this was accompanied by the feeling that your eyes were vibrating making focusing extremely difficult.

I was warned about the *Tiger Cape*, she was a mess. A small ship with three hatches, one 25-tonne and two 35-tonne electro hydraulic cranes, she was trading between Madras and Colombo. At the time I joined she was the worst ship I had ever seen, but unbelievably this has been surpassed in the last four years with ease. She was built in Lubeck in 1982 and was literally rotten. The Captain was a New Zealander, the

Chief Engineer German, the First Engineer was Croatian and the rest Philippino.

I flew from Heathrow to Delhi international then endured an uncomfortable bus ride to Delhi internal. Cows wandered about the streets and the whole place looked a complete disaster area. I then flew Sahara Indian Airways to Madras (Chennai) and spent the night in a most awful hotel. I washed my hands, but could detect a terrible smell, so I washed them again and it became worse. Turning the shower on was worse still – there had been floods and raw sewage had got into the fresh water system. My bags were lost and I had to borrow clothes, but not from the German Electrical Officer I replaced as he had some kind of skin problem that looked contagious even though I was assured it was not. I was relieved to get to my cabin on the ship, and eventually retrieved my bags 10 days later after British Airways had given me money to replace some clothing though in truth it was the fault of Sahara Indian an Airline I would never recommend. Breakfast in the hotel consisted of either rice with green or rice with brown – what this was made of I had no idea so I avoided it and went hungry.

It took forty-two hours to sail from Madras to Colombo; we did it the whole time I was on that ship, a most monotonous schedule.

The Chief Engineer was replaced by Graham Walker and things improved until my accident. I had told the Captain about the locking mechanism on a hatch, warning that it could fall. It did, on my head, and I ended up in a hospital in Colombo being stitched back together. We had received a new Captain that day who I had not realised disliked the sight of blood. I lost a lot and ended up with twenty-three stitches in my head. Ferdi the Croatian accompanied me to hospital and I was installed in a very basic room, not being wheeled to the operating theatre until the middle of the night. I refused to have a general anaesthetic and endured a lot of pain as injections were put into my head. I was glad they did as one cut had been missed and I was able to direct them to it. As I turned over I was amused to see that the orderly had no shoes yet the nurse and doctor did. As I was wheeled to my room in the early hours, the ward sister was obviously looking for someone. She passed by and I looked under my bed aware that all was not well; the orderly was hiding there, and I could not help but laugh.

The doctor was amazed that I wanted to return to my ship but as I pointed out the food and the accommodation were better and along with air conditioning I would be much better off. I would look up at the ceiling and watch fat lizards chase lazy flies; the place was very dirty but they did a good job of stitching up my head.

I returned to the ship and lived a very lonely life as few people had time to visit me, my stitches were taken out and I tried to take things as easy as possible. Christmas was spent in Colombo, dinner being a barbecue of turkey and suckling pig. At 0100 on Christmas morning I was working on #1 crane as it had failed. After I got it working I walked aft to find Ferdi scratching his head. As we were taking on fuel water was coming out of the ballast tank-sounding pipe. We later found out that the fuel lines passed through the ballast tanks and had holes in them. Fortunately no oil was spilled, Ferdi had caught it in time.

A repair firm were called in Madras. As the main power cables were in a pipe going through the same tank we made sure they knew not to cut out that pipe. Needless to say they did – in India it is normal to be ignored, they always think they know better.

Madras is not very nice, we employed a firm to clean out our oil tanks, and I saw children no older than ten years old enter dark oily

Christmas Day 1998 on MV Tiger, Cape Colombo, Sri Lanka. Ferdi (First Egineer) looks on whilst the Bosun sings karaoke

tanks completely naked. The Indians thought this was perfectly OK, although large posters adorned the docks extolling the virtues of safety equipment such as helmets, boots and gloves. There were two problems that I heard of: the first was that no one would pay for the equipment; the second was the argument that if they did the workers were so poor that they would sell it anyway. This way of thinking will keep India in a permanent state of chaos and therefore poor. I saw sights in Madras that appalled me – mothers washing their children in filthy puddles, the exploitation of children who are looked on as cheap labour and filth beyond belief. I also saw great wealth; as in other countries I have visited (such as Brazil) the wealth is held by a few. It could be better distributed and until the country stops testing nuclear armaments and starts looking after its people there is no hope for those people mentioned.

The time dragged on; my head was better though I did suffer from headaches for a while. We received a new Philippino Chief Officer who amused us at first but soon became a hazard. At a safety meeting when he was asked what improvements could be made to the vessel he said 'Noodles', the argument being that if the men were working late they might get tired and have an accident but would be OK if noodles were supplied. The next problem was a little more serious. On leaving Madras the Captain telephoned the control room and said that he had dropped the anchor because of a steering gear failure. We could find nothing wrong so I positioned myself on the bridge. We started off again, the Captain gave the order to go to port, and the helmsman put the wheel to starboard. He was removed and replaced by what should have been our senior deck officer; he did exactly the same thing. Eventually the Second Mate was called and he managed to steer us out.

The company was experiencing problems, crane drivers in Colombo were wrecking the cranes so the company sent us two Philippino crane drivers. On joining one of them turned white when he was told he was a crane driver, informing us that the last time he drove one he nearly killed somebody. When attending a crane one night in Colombo I was attacked by a Sri Lankan crane driver; the Foremen sent him off the job and explained that he was a problem as he had a drug habit. I complained to the Captain (the third captain in three months) who chose to do nothing, so I resigned on the spot.

I eventually left the ship two weeks later in Colombo, relieved by the Electrical Officer who had walked off the *Saga Rose*. His description of that ship was not good and as the company had lost the contract for the APL ships, it was obvious where I would be needed. Added to that, as we were paid in Deutsch marks and the exchange rate was getting to be unfavourable for us my money was going down. I resolved to look elsewhere.

The trip through Colombo to the airport passed through several checkpoints as the Tamils were systematically destroying the place with bombs. One of the best hotels had been blown up while we were travelling to Colombo. At the anchorage patrol boats constantly swept the area on the lookout for pirates. Prior to my arrival the ship had been attacked by pirates, who had plundered a container.

In Colombo a ship was under repair because the Sri Lankan Air Force had attacked it by mistake. The proximity of these people in boats bristling with guns did not boost my confidence, being aware that they were as likely to shoot us by mistake as any pirates.

I left the company and drew all of my leave pay; as usual they were upset at me leaving, the personnel officer particularly so. All I can say to those people is that they did not have to live in those conditions with diminishing pay. Promised pay rises to compensate did not materialise. Most companies are now struggling to find trained personnel and it is only natural that in this climate people will pick and choose whom they work for. In the late 1980's officers and crew had to beg for a job and companies were ruthless with terms and conditions. Now due to a lack of investment in training those companies who relied on cheap labour are in trouble. If you choose to employ someone from a country where there is no free education and corruption is rife, where fraud, falsification of documents and bribery is a way of life, then problems on ships will increase. It may take some time to show depending on the individuals concerned.

On the *Tiger Cape* in a small crew of under twenty I saw five nationalities; we were lucky that Ferdi the Croatian spoke reasonable English; we were also lucky to have some experienced Philippinos, especially the Bosun. The Bosun would barter for fish when at anchor with bottles of whiskey. People would surround the ship in canoes made out of trees tied together with an outboard motor on. He used to constantly ask for empty bottles, and I found out later that he used to fill the empty whiskey bottles with cold tea, then swap them for fish.

CHAPTER XI

Training and Tankers

MY PRESENT EMPLOYMENT is my first shore-based job. I still go on ships but for the first time I have no emergency station, no fire-fighting responsibilities and am constantly hopping from one ship to another, never getting the time to feel like a member of the crew. Some of the ships I attend have French officers with a French flag, the rest Norwegian and it is my first departure from a ship-based life. I know more about the company than any other I have worked for, seeing at first hand the difficulties shore staff experience. That is why I can write this objectively, applying what I know now to what has happened in the past. The company is based in Norway and deals almost exclusively in Europe.

For a few months I worked for this Norwegian shipping company on a self-employed basis. I started this in April 1998 until June when I was persuaded to join what I still think of as the worst ship I have ever had the misfortune to serve on. At the same time my eldest son David had joined the MV *British Steel* a 90,000-tonne bulk carrier. As Trinity House does not have too many vessels it lends its cadets out to other companies. This would be fine if chief engineers and captains were able or trained to cope with trainees. Unfortunately all too many of these senior officers treat cadets as cheap labour or have nothing to do with them.

A Second Engineer once complained to me about a cadet who could do nothing, knew nothing and was a waste of time. I pointed out to him that the cadet was only sixteen years old and had never seen a ship in his life. That particular ship was in dry dock and everything in the engine room was in thousands of pieces, so I advised the cadet to touch nothing without being told. That particular ship had two British, one Norwegian, one Danish Officer and a Portuguese crew, four nationalities in a crew of twelve.

During this time my youngest son, Michael, joined Maersk Line, a

Michael at sea with Maersk

Danish shipping company, in September 1998 following the trail to sea. He also enrolled in South Shields college. Knowing the state of the industry and the inadequate training given I was a little apprehensive and in fact advised them both to seek alternative employment. My eldest son had a BTec Diploma in automobile engineering and I had thought that he would follow that path. My experiences and injuries coupled by long periods spent away from the comforts of home should have been enough of a deterrent. It must be something in the brain, an aberration, as my friend Bill Fogarty's sons are both in South Shields college and I would not be surprised if his third son joins as well.

    The training needs to be updated, many of the instructors have not been to sea for a long time and others have not been to sea at all. I helped my sons with the electrical content and was amazed to see that they were being taught about things that no longer existed and they were unlikely to see. It is small wonder that many engineers are confused when confronted with a modern electrical drawing, symbols have changed as have methods of drawing. The course is not extensive enough to adequately teach good theory and therefore engineers should be familiarised with what will confront them in the real world. At sea there is

My Family.
Left to right: Myself; John (father); Gwen (wife); Michael (son); Enid (mother); David (son)

no one to help, you are on your own. In these days of cheap international crew and reduced manning this has never been truer than now.

The *British Steel* had the usual mixture of nationalities, a Turkish Chief Officer and eventually Branko who had sailed with me on the *Snow Flower*. Branko, determined to do me a favour, resolved to make David's life hard. He told me that if his sons showed an interest in a life at sea he would break their legs; he was definitely not joking. David joined the ship in Swansea and sailed to Sept Iles (seven islands) and Port Cartier in Canada. This run continued back and forth across the Atlantic with a cargo of iron ore. Cracks appeared in the decks and from what I know of old ships carrying heavy cargo I was glad when he got off it. There has been much written about bulk carriers and the fate of ships such as the *Derbyshire* and *Kowloon Bridge* (both built in the UK) has been the subject of a lot of debate. For those readers who are not familiar with the story of those ships, they both sank and in the case of the *Derbyshire* with all hands. He finished his trip by going to Saldanha Bay where we had both been in 1996, and paid off in Redcar. My wife picked him up and described the red dust that covered everything including the car.

His next ship was a steam tanker owned by BP, the *British Ranger*, yet again an aging ship, due for scrap in one year with the ship's staff fearful of losing their jobs. This is no climate to send a cadet; it is not surprising that he describes them as cynical. They went from the Philippines to the Gulf and he paid off in Suez. There was already a smattering of Polish officers and there was no feeling of permanence. He was often told that there was no point in training him as he was not a BP cadet, a very short-sighted attitude but sadly all too common in what is loosely described as the Merchant Navy.

Other ships he was sent to for small periods of time were the THV *Mermaid*, MV *Pacific Pintail* and the MV *Celandine*. The *Mermaid*, owned and operated by Trinity House, this was a well-run and happy ship; most people had spent a long time in Trinity House and this was one of the few ships that he sailed on where I felt he had actually learned something. The *Pacific Pintail* runs from Barrow to Japan to collect nuclear waste for reprocessing but he stayed in Barrow. The MV *Celandine* was another matter. Despite flying the Red Ensign the only Brit was the Captain, the Chief Engineer being Belgian and most of the others Polish. When sending a cadet on a ship to learn it would be helpful if everyone spoke the same language.

TRAINING AND TANKERS

After three years he took and passed his fourth class engineer's certificate and at the time of writing is serving on the *Maersk Gosport*, a container vessel, and I hear from him occasionally, most recently from Portsmouth, Virginia. Watching cadets in my own company it is surprising that anyone stays to the end and a significant number do not.

My youngest son Michael served on two gas tankers, the *Maersk Suffolk* and the *Maersk Sussex* as an engine cadet but after two years decided that the sea was not for him. The fact that he had an accident, which resulted from a chain block hitting him on the head, and then to read later that there had been no accidents on the ship, did not help. He describes the smell of gas in the engine room when taking on cargo and although he had some good times ashore in Spain, the Mississippi, Houston, Mexico and Turkey, he does not regret his decision. He has already seen more of the world than most other people and the experiences he had can contribute to his own book in later life.

While all of this was going on I had agreed to join a product tanker called the *Asphalt Navigator* much to the annoyance of the Norwegian company. The new company informed me that she was a mess; they were not wrong. The company I worked for only had the manning, it was actually owned by Sergeant Marine, an American company who specialised in the transportation of asphalt. They had, with a total lack of imagination, named their ships *Asphalt Victory*, *Asphalt Commodore* etc.

I had to join the ship in Las Palmas where she had undergone a dry dock of several weeks. There were four Brits, a Pole, an Indonesian, six Bulgarian fitters and a Philippino crew. The Chief Engineer, Reg Cummins, has become a good friend due to our combined efforts to make some sense of the madness that prevailed. The electricians were thought of as useless but when I saw the tools they had to work with I was not surprised that they could achieve little.

When carrying asphalt it is necessary to keep it heated otherwise it solidifies into a hard lump that has to be dug out. To do this there were three boilers that pumped heated thermal oil through pipes to the different tanks. Two cargo pumps were our only method of discharging the cargo; they were in a separate pump room driven from two-speed electric motors in the engine room.

I started to look around and soon saw that we had a mammoth task on our hands; Reg had already warned me about what I would find. To be fair the company tried its hardest to solve the problems but each problem masked another. There were extra people everywhere including two Danish electricians who were excellent, but I am afraid not in possession of a magic wand, any more than I was.

The American Superintendent took me ashore to buy tools after a heated exchange on the subject. Holes were found in the tanks and we were delayed longer while these were repaired. He described the ship as 'a peach'. I soon disabused him of this odd notion, as my cabin was filthy, I could not flush the toilet, the galley was a mess and the officers' mess resembled a poor version of a 'greasy spoon café'.

I had been under the impression that the ship would be repaired before we set sail. Two things then happened which made me realise the awful truth. The arrival of the company QA representative who turned out to be an ex-officer in the US Coastguard, followed by an Englishman (ex-RN) from our own MCA (Marine Coastguard Agency). When I was interviewed along with the other officers, I pointed out that we had no planned maintenance system and that virtually every system on the ship was in a poor state of repair. I still have photographs of lifeboats held up by wires and chain blocks, impossible to launch. They remained in that state until after I left the ship two and a half months later. The Chief Engineer also pointed out several major problems that the vessel faced. When we were issued with an ISO standard and passed the inspection, I was and remain shocked. At this point I would like to add that the same man from the MCA arrested a ship I was on in Southampton in October that year with far fewer problems.

On leaving Las Palmas we encountered problems immediately – the steering gear failed, the main engine refused to go astern and there was no remote control. The Lloyds surveyor witnessed me answering the telegraph, run out to the upper platform and shout to the Chief at the engine control stand (usually only used in emergency), then point for'd or aft to signify ahead or astern then at my foot for dead slow, knee for slow, etc. ending at my head for full as there was no telegraph fitted at the control stand. We soon found that we had no astern movement, a hydraulic motor on the cam being defective. I managed to repair the steering gear and rig up the remote stops on the generators to the satisfaction of the surveyor. Awful noises came from the engine but the surveyor seemed to want the ship to go. The pilot on being told we had no astern movement said that he knew of the problem, as he had been

TRAINING AND TANKERS

the Captain of the ship six years previously. How we got to the terminal in Tenerife is beyond me. We loaded asphalt for Nigeria then, using a tug as our astern movement, left Tenerife on our way to Port Harcourt.

The voyage from Capetown to Antwerp used to take about two weeks, but we took three weeks to get from the Canary Islands to Nigeria. I noticed a stream of oil at one point going over the side, which eventually stopped, but only after two days; I have no idea where it came from. One morning the engine stopped, so did the boilers, a fuel problem caused by a mistake in transferring. It took several hours to clean sludge from the boiler nozzles, which resulted in the cargo cooling, something that was to cause us a lot of problems in the future.

We approached the Bonny River with apprehension, manoeuvring would be difficult in the limited space of the river. We edged forward, aware that there had been a coup in Nigeria. At night we stopped and attempted to discharge 2,000 tonnes of cargo into a barge. The first pump caught fire as the Chief Officer tried to run it at high speed, having been advised not to as we knew that the asphalt was cooler than it should be and therefore thicker. The pump was wrecked so he started the other pump, also at high speed, and the starter box in the engine room blew up. I repaired it in two hours and we gradually started pumping.

That night boats appeared and the ship was overrun with local girls and bottles of all kinds of alcohol. The next morning we started again, when suddenly the Captain stopped the ship and dropped the anchor. We still had no astern movement and no chance of fixing it. He was persuaded to resume with a tug as our astern movement, and we arrived at Port Harcourt in the evening. There were people with AK47 assault rifles wandering around the ship and two engineers were arrested at the main gate when trying to go ashore for some relaxation. I had declined the offer of a night ashore and was very pleased I remained onboard.

We discharged through a pipeline up a jetty. At one point a part of the jetty which had a mobile crane on it collapsed and people ran around shouting. One man shouted at me to do something, but there was of course nothing to do without heavy lift equipment to pull the crane out and shore up the jetty. It was their own lack of maintenance and disorganisation that was to blame, not our ship.

The full scale of the problem was brought home to me while talking to the director of the repair firm Ken Oki who had come to resolve our lifeboat davit problem (we were still unable to launch our lifeboats). He told me a tale of woe and the impossibility of running anything properly in Nigeria. He was both educated and eloquent. I was informed that anything ordered from Lagos was unlikely to arrive in Port Harcourt as it would be stolen along the way, his men had neither tools nor materials yet managed to work with enthusiasm and ingenuity. It is not surprising that their repair did not last long and we were reduced to having to tie the lifeboats up with chain blocks again.

The Americans blamed the management company for all of these problems but in truth it was a combination of factors. The ship had been built in Spain in 1982. I have worked on three ships all built in the same yard at about the same time; all were of inferior quality, the other two have been scrapped. The problems with the main engine were long standing but not addressed in dry dock despite the fact that we had a B&W representative on site. The company could do no more than listen to the maker's rep; it was also unlikely that the problem would go away. By issuing the ship with an ISO certificate this put pressure on the Lloyds surveyor, who knew that our company could ask Lloyds why the ship was detained when it had been certified by the British MCA. It is likely that he would have been forced to pass the ship; he told me that he would be glad when we left port.

We limped back down the Bonny River and on the way out I received a telex from my wife to say that a job had been offered to me from my present company. I informed the manning company who could not match the offer and so I resigned. Howls of righteous indignation followed by a letter stating that my resignation was viewed with disappointment as they had warned me of the state of the vessel. All they had to do was offer me a better contract but they failed miserably.

Resigning and leaving are two different things; we called into Freetown, Sierra Leone to pick up another service engineer, the Captain being the only man who thought that we would leave in a different condition. We anchored offshore; when the boat returned with the service engineer to go to the airport we still had no astern movement.

We limped on to Cadiz and upon tying up were duly arrested for non-payment of dry dock fees. This period of dry-dock benefited the ship but she was still a mess and I predicted that she would sink. A new Chief Engineer relieved Reg and more repairs were carried out. It was discovered that the turbo charger for the main engine was the wrong kind, and that was only one problem. A Swedish Superintendent had arrived; I decided to go for a few beers after being told the ship would remain for another week. When I returned the ship had sailed and I spent the night at the dock police gate. Next day I was driven to Algeciras and met the ship by boat along with a turbo charger specialist.

I left the ship on 9 September 1998 at Tarragona by boat; I was then whisked to Barcelona Airport and flew home. That is not the end of the saga – in October 1999 whilst walking with my son through South Shields I met the Captain of that ship. He had sailed into a port in Mexico, the engine failed, they were unable to start it and the ship had strayed onto the rocks putting eighteen 3-metre holes in the ship's bottom. She did not totally sink as the water was shallow but she stayed for some time. I later heard that she had been raised and was once again trading; it is likely that disaster will follow that ship wherever she goes, wrecking careers and polluting the oceans. We can only hope that no one is killed.

The MCA inspector looked totally relaxed when I challenged him over his decisions concerning that ship, which in my opinion were at best ill advised.

CHAPTER XII

Ashore

I HAVE NOW WORKED in my shore-based position for three years and I have attended ships in dry dock at Bazan (near Cadiz in Spain), Bremerhaven, Teesport, Santander, Falmouth and most recently Barcelona. There have been few highlights and the work is often mundane and not worthy of comment. It is for this reason that I will pick out only those voyages and ships of which I have something positive to say. I am required to write lengthy reports on all of the ships' electrical systems, spending two to three weeks of each year on every vessel and I am heartily sick of writing about them.

When I started I was the only electrical specialist for eighteen ships. The company relied heavily on contractors and it did not take long to find out that some people were taking advantage of this. There are now four people in the department for fewer ships and I believe that this has resulted in a significant improvement for the company, reducing costs and moving from a fire-fighting mentality to a more considered approach, taking into account future needs such as maintenance instead of fix and go.

Most of the ships are Norwegian flagged with five French-flagged vessels. Of these three were built in Japan in 2000, four in the Netherlands between 1996 and 1999, one in Norway in 1992 and the rest of various vintage from 1977 onwards.

I have made many friends on the ships and probably a few enemies – no one likes an outsider coming onto their ship and writing down defects, especially some of the older engineers. Some would have me believe that their ships are perfect and nothing needs to be done; if I ever find such a ship I will be very surprised indeed.

Since joining this company I have had the pleasure of attending two new buildings. The first in Harlingen was not so memorable, the second was a different story altogether.

MV Autosun in Tsuneishi, Japan, December 2000

In December 2000 I flew from Newcastle airport to Amsterdam then on to Osaka. Taking the bullet train from Kobe to Fukuyama I was met by the agent and taken to a hotel in Tsuneishi. The hotel was clean and comfortable, but there were some strange things on the menu like crab brains and deep-fried snapper guts. The shipyard is very productive and it was here that I first saw the MV *Autosun*, our third and final build.

She is a car carrier of 20,000 tonnes with two main engines to give a service speed of around 22 knots. There are twin stabilisers and a good generating plant. There were problems leaving Tsuneishi because of steering gear faults, but I cured the electrical ones, which were mainly loose connections between the autopilot and the steering system. We sailed from Tsuneishi taking in two ports in Japan and then on to Laembechang in Thailand where we stayed for three hours.

We then sailed to an anchorage off Singapore to take on fuel, which took a few hours, then sailed on to Suez. It was reported that there had been a pirate attack in the anchorage we were in and the pirates had robbed the crew. They would have been sadly disappointed with me as

ASHORE

I carry little of value with me to sea – old clothes and battered boots, my only valued possession being my mouth organ, which can now barely issue a note. I carry personal photographs and an old CD player, a paltry haul indeed.

There were a few small problems whilst I was on the ship but few worthy of comment. The company asked me to leave the ship in Suez, a boat took me off, then a taxi carried me to Cairo and an altogether different standard to the one in Japan.

I flew Air France from Cairo to Paris then Heathrow to Newcastle on 6 January 2001; my bags arrived four days later. I knew then that my time at sea was just about at an end and I am seeking pastures new. The ship was in the capable hands of Gareth Griffiths; an experienced Chief Engineer ably assisted by the First Engineer Johnny Holland and the Third Engineer Chas Cummings. They are a good team and I wish them well, we had a very pleasant trip across the Indian Ocean with Christmas and New Year being a low key but still enjoyable celebration.

This voyage brings us up to the present; I was on one of our French ships, the MV *Montlhery* writing in my scrapbook in my spare time when the Second Engineer Jean Pierre Yven asked me if I would be mentioning him. He is a Breton from Brittany who has served in the French Navy and seemingly not French at all. A jolly round fellow with a beard and an infectious grin he is very hard to ignore or dislike. Some of the French have given me a rough ride but JP2, as he is known, has always been most helpful. Both he and the Captain, Claude Lancou, own small fishing boats in the same town and they confuse all around by talking in a mish mash of French, Breton and English. They showed me a video of the places they go fishing and with waves crashing on rocks only a few metres from their boats I am quite sure that they are both mad. The Captain on the other French vessel, Dominique Thos, has also helped me in what can sometimes be a very hostile situation. Luckily the Superintendent, Brian Anderson, has sailed with the French on many occasions and has an understanding of them without which we would be lost indeed.

It is not easy to sit at a dinner table night after night and not be able to converse. Having served with several nationalities I know the problems and know of several people who have had nervous breakdowns because of this feeling of isolation. When in a mess with predominantly British

Indian Ocean. From Left: Dennis (Second Mate); Gareth Griffiths (Chief Engineer); Johnny Holland (First Engineer); Chas Cummings (Third Engineer)

I try to include minorities in the conversation, that is good manners and sadly it is lacking in most merchant vessels.

I have now worked on fifteen of the company's vessels, two of which have been scrapped. Everyone moans about his or her employer but as I said to someone in this company, 'This is as good as it gets at sea.' I know of no other company that is better. That is the reason I am trying to get a job that does not involve shipping companies as in general they are not nice people to work for. Ships cost money, to upkeep them costs money. The reason for most of the problems I have experienced is a desire to cut costs on crew, equipment and maintenance; put those three things together and you have a disaster waiting to happen.

We are as a nation dependent on the sea, our economy depends on it, but ask any shopper in a supermarket where their apples have come from, or coffee and tea, and you get a blank look. People often ask me what is the difference between the Royal Navy and the Merchant Navy. I just smile these days, they wouldn't believe me if I told them. That there are thousands of seamen from hundreds of countries thrown together for the sake of making money would be a simple answer. I have sailed with people from twenty-four nations that I can remember; the list may be greater. With such a huge number of people co-operating together in often difficult conditions it seems ridiculous to go back to our respective countries only to find ourselves at war with each other. However wars are not about nationality or individuals, they are about power and differing ideologies, things that the average seaman has little interest in. The war in the Falklands ultimately defeated a vicious fascist government, as did the war against Hitler. When at war we can only hope that we are on the side of the righteous and be thankful that we have young people in the armed services prepared to defend what this nation stands for.

List of Subscribers

Andrew Young, Berwickshire

Margaret Nicholas, Kelty

Peter Ostick, Coventry

Bernard and Elizabeth Bamford, Hartley

Mr J.E. King, Dover

Mr Martin Parry, Cramlington

Samantha Dixon, Bedlington

Michael Hegarty MNI MCIT MILT, Co. Donegal

Mr Ivan Gillespie, Co. Londonderry

Frank Allison, Kirkby Stephen

Stephen John Jarrett, Northampton

Allan Hargrave Jarrett, Northampton

Malcolm Noble, Cramlington

Mr Nigel White, Grimsby

Enid and John Nicholas, Kirkby Stephen

Joyce Goodwin, Orpington

Daphne Higgins, Rochester

J.A.B. Dickie, Dunfermline

Mrs Jean C. Howe, Bedlington

Captain Gavin J. Swadel MN, Dundee

Mr G.A. Walker, Bradford

John Lusher, Ashington

Capt. Ken Thorpe, Hornsea

Mr Iain S. Voller, USA

Dr. Walter Jones, USA

Claude Lancou, Primelin, France

Jean-Luc Remond, Perros-Guirec, France

Ken Sharpe, Cleethorpes

Chris Dring, Cleethorpes

Mr J.N. Howard, Driffield

'Babsy' Ridley, Boldon Colliery

John Convery, Blaydon

David Nicholas, Bedlington

Beverley Nicholas, Bedlington

William G. Fogarty, Dover

Einar Myrseth, Grimstad, Norway

G. Griffiths, York

Sue Jennings, Bedlington

Ian Paterson, Sunderland

Dennis John Ayling, Bishop Auckland

LIST OF SUBSCRIBERS

Thomas Westerlund, Hestra, Sweden

Mark Sword, Morpeth

Dirk Daems, Antwerp, Belgium

Jeremy and Angela Higgins, Gillingham

Dieter Roeben, Hinte, Germany

Malcolm M. Thomson, Whitley Bay

Theresa Kennedy, River Dover

Emma Kennedy, River Dover

Black & Grey Public House, Morpeth

Philip McClarence, Morpeth

Wendy Irving, Dover

Les Powell, Adisham

Thomas Robert Gelder, New York, North Shields

Brian Anderson, Hogsthorpe

Peter Griffin, Solihull

Mr M.A. Helps, Corby

Dr R.A. Moody, Irthlingborough

Janet Spencer, Boldon

Leanne Spencer, Boldon

Mr Norman Langdon, Torrington

M. Trolan, Morpeth

Mr A.J. Simpson, Otley